TALES FROM THE INDIANAPOLIS COLTS SIDELINE

TALES FROM THE

INDIANAPOLIS COLTS SIDELINE

A COLLECTION OF THE GREATEST COLTS STORIES EVER TOLD

BY
MIKE CHAPPELL
AND
PHIL RICHARDS

SPORTS
PUBLISHING

Sports Publishing books may be purchased in bulk at special discounts for sales promotion, corporate gifts, fund-raising, or educational purposes. Special editions can also be created to specifications. For details, contact the Special Sales Department, Sports Publishing, 307 West 36th Street, 11th Floor, New York, NY 10018 or sportspubbooks@skyhorsepublishing.com.

Sports Publishing® is a registered trademark of Skyhorse Publishing, Inc.®, a Delaware corporation.

Visit our website at www.sportspubbooks.com.

10 9 8 7 6 5 4 3 2

Library of Congress Cataloging-in-Publication Data is available on file.

Cover design by Tom Lau
Cover photo: AP Images

ISBN: 978-1-68358-161-1
Ebook ISBN: 978-1-68358-167-3

Printed in the United States of America

Contents

Introduction

The evolution began in March 1984, under the cover of darkness on a snowy night in Owings Mills, Maryland. Owner Robert Irsay, unable to convince Baltimore city officials to build him a new stadium, and fearful of an "imminent domain" takeover, brought in Mayflower vans and moved his franchise to Indianapolis. It was a slow, fitful process, one that took more than two decades to achieve the ultimate objective—a world championship after the 2006 season—and one that has involved 11 head/interim coaches.

But the nomadic Colts, once so integral to the Baltimore landscape and culture, now have deep roots in Indianapolis. They emerged from those frustrating early years in Indiana as new kids on the sports block with no real unifying identity to perennial NFL powerhouse.

The franchise that forced its fan base to endure a 4-12 Indy debut in 1984 and a 1-15 season in 1991 rewarded it with a victory over the Chicago Bears in Super Bowl XLI and a near-miss against the New Orleans Saints in Super Bowl XLIV three years later.

So much to celebrate.

The catalyst was the selection of quarterback Peyton Manning with the first overall pick in the 1998 draft. It delivered a future Hall of Famer to a roster that lacked star power. There were two trips to the Super Bowl in a four-year stretch. Nine consecutive playoff appearances, tying the Dallas Cowboys for the longest streak in NFL history. From 2000 through 2009, 115 regular-season victories, the most by any team in any decade in league history.

And, lately, so much change.

From Bill Polian to Ryan Grigson.

From Jim Caldwell to Chuck Pagano.
From Peyton Manning to Andrew Luck.
From Ryan Grigson to Chris Ballard.
From 8-8 in 2016 to . . . what?

Chapter One

STARTING OVER

The date is open to debate.

January 1, 2012? That's when the Colts dropped a 19-13 decision at Jacksonville, finished 2011 with a 2-14 record and secured the first overall pick in the April draft.

March 7, 2012? That's when owner Jim Irsay decided not to pay a $28 million option bonus to iconic, ailing quarterback Peyton Manning, making the NFL's only four-time MVP an unrestricted free agent.

April 26, 2012? That's when the torch officially was passed. With the No. 1 overall pick in the NFL draft, Andrew Luck of Stanford was a Colt.

Never mind the timeline. The end game was undeniable.

The next era of the Colts was ushered in when Irsay decided the time was right to transition from Manning, for so long the franchise's face and catalyst, to Luck, considered the best quarterback prospect coming out of college since, well, Peyton Manning in 1998.

"I couldn't be more excited," Irsay said. "I think that we are really blessed as a franchise to have such a player and such a person. All of the things that Andrew brings to Indianapolis and to the Colts is really special."

Throughout the evaluation process—Luck or Baylor QB Robert Griffin III?—Irsay received the similar input from personnel experts.

"The comment you always got from them was, 'He is the best player I've scouted in 25 years. He is the top prospect I've graded in 20 years,'" Irsay said.

On April 26, 2012, Quarterback Andrew Luck became a member of the Colts. (AP Photo)

"We are really fortunate as a franchise to have him. We are really excited about this new era, and we look forward to doing great things as we go forward in this decade."

Luck, twice a runner-up in the Heisman Trophy voting, embraced the opportunity Indianapolis was offering.

"There is such a great history of winning," he said. "I know that I will work my butt off to try and make sure that the team is in a position to win as many games as it can."

The Season

The baseline for expectations always had been winning the AFC South and reaching the playoffs.

That changed in September 2011 when it was announced Manning's streak of 227 consecutive starts, including the playoffs, would end. Four neck procedures in a 19-month stretch were too much even for Manning, who had missed just one snap due to injury over the previous 13 seasons, to overcome.

Life went on, albeit with a dramatically different flow.

"However it shakes down—whoever's available and ready—we've got to go play," Jeff Saturday, Manning's long-time center/friend, said. "I don't think the Texans are going to take it easy on us because somebody's not playing."

For the first time since the final game of the 1997 season, someone other than Manning started for the Colts in their opener at Houston. Kerry Collins was ineffective and roughed up in a 34-7 loss that was every bit as lopsided as it appeared.

As Manning watched, first from the coaches' box and then from the sidelines, the weeks passed, quarterbacks changed and the losses mounted. The Colts became just the seventh team since 1960 to open a season with 13 losses.

Backup Curtis Painter replaced Collins, lost nine starts and was replaced by Dan Orlovsky. It was Orlovsky who finally got the job done. He led the Colts to wins over Tennessee and Houston before the season-ending loss at Jacksonville that secured the first overall pick in the draft and, hopefully, the key to the future.

"We'll see how it all shakes out and obviously none of us in this room are in control," Saturday said as he sat at his cubicle long after the loss to the Jaguars. "Mr. Irsay is going to handle all of that."

Manning held court as his teammates showered, dressed, filed out.

"It's been hard not being able to help this year on the field," he said.

The Overhaul

The season was long, arduous, unproductive.

Irsay acted swiftly.

A day after the loss in Jacksonville, he fired vice chairman Bill Polian and general manager Chris Polian.

"I have always believed it's about timing, it's about energy, it's about what the time calls for," Irsay said.

On Polian's 14-season watch, the Colts reached the playoffs 11 times, the Super Bowl twice. They won a world championship after the 2006 season against the Bears in a steady south Florida rain but lost another three years later on the same site against the New Orleans Saints.

Enough was enough after Irsay saw his proud organization deal with a 13-game losing streak to open 2011 en route to a 2-14 mark. Jobs were at stake, and lost.

"Intuitive decision," Irsay insisted of parting ways with Polian and his son. "Clearly we are in a rebuilding stage."

That continued less than two weeks later when Irsay named Ryan Grigson his next general manager.

It intensified when the decision was reached to fire coach Jim Caldwell and replace him with Baltimore Ravens defensive coordinator Chuck Pagano.

The massive restructuring of the franchise's leadership was complete.

"It's still about getting the best players, the best coaches and having leaders and people that inspire the organization to go out and compete at the highest level," reasoned Irsay.

The Goodbye

Suspense was lacking when Irsay and Manning walked behind a podium in the team's auditorium on March 7, 2012. Media filled rows of chairs. Team employees ringed the room, two, three layers thick.

Everyone knew the occasion. Nearly 14 years after Irsay and Manning shared the stage to herald a new beginning, they stood side by side to announce the end.

The team would not pick up a $28 million option bonus due Manning. The person most responsible for an on-field transformation from NFL afterthought to NFL relevance was an unrestricted free agent.

Irsay appeared shaken as he spoke. Frequently, his voice broke with emotion.

"It's a difficult day of shared pain between Peyton, myself, the fans, everyone," Irsay said. "The good times we've had together, the laughs we've shared together."

He paused, regrouped.

"You know, when a 37-year-old owner met a 22-year-old player coming out of Tennessee and the dreams that we had and experienced are just beyond my imagination. He's always a part of the horseshoe. I can't thank him enough."

The foundation of Manning's career had been preparation. He was ready for one of the most difficult moments of his athletic life. He read a prepared statement that was anything but impassive.

"I sure have loved playing football for the Indianapolis Colts," Manning began, his eyes darting from the paper to the crowd. "For 14 wonderful years . . ."

Like Irsay, Manning paused, gathered himself.

"I've been a Colt for almost all of my adult life," he finally continued. "But I guess in life and in sports, we all know that nothing lasts forever. Times change. Circumstances change, and that's the reality of playing in the NFL.

"I haven't thought a lot about where I'll play, but I have thought about where I've been and I've truly been blessed to play here. I've been blessed to play in the NFL and as I go, I go with just a few words left to say, a few words I want to address to Colts fans everywhere."

There were a few moist eyes in the crowd. That soon increased.

"Thank you very much from the bottom of my heart," Manning said. "I truly have enjoyed being your quarterback."

Complete Housecleaning

Manning's departure was the one that reverberated loudest across the NFL, but the roster purge hardly ended with the much-decorated QB.

Also caught up in the housecleaning were tight end Dallas Clark, running back Joseph Addai, linebacker and defensive captain Gary Brackett and safety Melvin Bullitt, cap casualties all. Grigson decided to re-sign veterans Reggie Wayne and Robert Mathis, but allowed center Jeff Saturday, wide receiver Pierre Garcon and tight end Jacob Tamme to hit the free agent market.

Saturday signed with Green Bay, Garcon landed in Washington and Tamme relocated to Denver. There, Tamme was reunited with Manning, who signed a five-year, $96 million contract with John Elway's Broncos.

"It's been a surprise every day," Wayne said. "You just take it in stride."

The New Guy

It's impossible not to connect the dots.

As a youngster, Luck attended the Manning Passing Academy in Louisiana. While at Stanford, he served as a camp counselor. Oliver Luck, Andrew's father, and Archie Manning, Peyton's father, were teammates for portions of two seasons with the Houston Oilers.

"I've had a chance to talk with Peyton over the summers and I've called him," Luck said. "I called him and asked for his advice after I decided to come back to school. He was great; very informative, easy to talk to."

Manning, tongue firmly planted in his cheek, took credit for Luck being selected with the first overall pick in the draft. "Andrew attended our camp," he said, "which I think is really the reason he was the first pick in the draft, because of the coaching he got as a camper way back in the day."

On a more serious note, Manning envisioned a successful union.

"I think he'll fit in perfectly," he said. "He's a great player. He's a great kid."

Luck returned fire, so to speak.

"What he did is, obviously, legendary for this city and for the state," he said. "I know that if I woke up every morning trying to compare myself to Peyton, I think I would go crazy. It's impossible.

"I realize that, so I'm going to go out there and do the best I can. I'm going to put my best foot forward and if one day I can be mentioned alongside Peyton in quarterback lore, it would be a football dream come true."

There's one more eerie connection.

At Stanford, Luck played for coach Jim Harbaugh, who was the Colts' starting quarterback from 1994 to 1997. Harbaugh was traded prior to the 1998 draft to make way for Manning. Fourteen years later, Manning was released to make way for Luck.

The immediate Manning-to-Luck transition was beyond smooth and exceeded anyone's realistic expectations. In the first three seasons of the Luck era, the Colts posted identical 11-5 records and reached the playoffs each year. More than that, they advanced a step further each season and reached the AFC championship game after the 2014 campaign.

In short order, Luck established himself as one of the NFL's rising stars. His 12,957 passing yards were the most by a quarterback in his first three seasons and his 86 touchdown passes were second to Dan Marino's 98. Luck appeared in the Pro Bowl each season, and in '14 set a franchise record with 4,761 passing yards and led the league with 40 TD passes.

Then, the arrow leveled off as Luck dealt with a variety of injuries, an ever-changing and inconsistent offensive line and unreliable defense. He missed nine starts in 2015 with a lacerated kidney and injuries to his right shoulder and ribs, and missed one start in '16 with a concussion.

Suddenly Luck's star dimmed, and the Colts followed suit. They endured 8-8 records in 2015 and '16 and failed to make the playoffs in consecutive seasons for the first time since 1997–98.

Any doubt whether Luck would continue to lead the franchise were erased June 29, 2016, when owner Jim Irsay signed him to a five-year extension that made Luck the highest-paid player in NFL history. The deal tied Luck to the Colts through the 2021 season and would pay him nearly $140 million.

Luck dismissed the idea the hefty contract increased the pressure and expectations associated with him.

"I don't think so," he said. "I've always had very high expectations for myself; probably higher than what other people expect. As far as pressure, I think pressure is a privilege, and pressure from a coach, from your teammates, from your close friends and family is what's important to me.

"You can't control what folks are going to say good or bad, so I've never got too caught up in that."

The immediate fallout from failing to reach the playoffs in back-to-back seasons involved Irsay firing general manager Ryan Grigson and replacing him with Chris Ballard.

Chapter Two

SUPER AT LAST

Super At Last

There were a couple of oh-so-close moments, but the Super Bowl remained out of reach for the Colts until arguably the most scintillating, significant moment in their Indy era.

When cornerback Marlin Jackson hugged a Tom Brady interception and slid to the ground January 21, 2007, to secure a 38-34 victory over the hated New England Patriots in the AFC championship game, the Colts were headed to their first Super Bowl in 34 years.

"Obviously, there's a lot of emotion in the locker room," said coach Tony Dungy. "I've never been prouder. We had to go through a champion and we were down 18 points to them."

Down 21-3 in the second quarter and 21-6 at the half, the Manning-led Colts staged the biggest comeback in conference championship game history. Manning directed the game-winning drive with 2 minutes, 17 seconds remaining. Running back Joseph Addai provided the go-ahead 3-yard touchdown run behind center Jeff Saturday's pancake block of defensive tackle Vince Wilfork.

Jackson applied the exclamation point.

On to Miami.

Rain? What Rain?

History was made and an onerous monkey extricated from Peyton Manning's back on a rainy night in South Florida.

The Colts and Chicago Bears, separated by 185 miles in the country's heartland, met on February 4, 2007, at Dolphin Stadium for Super Bowl XLI. Tony Dungy joked the teams could have found a more convenient site, such as Fort Wayne, Indiana.

As it turned out, Dolphin Stadium was more than hospitable.

The Colts handled the Bears 29-17 in a game that began with Devin Hester's 92-yard kickoff return for a Chicago touchdown and essentially ended with cornerback Kelvin Hayden's 56-yard touchdown following an interception of a Rex Grossman pass.

It unfolded on a world-wide stage and in a steady rain. At game's end:

Dungy was the first black head coach to win a Super Bowl.

Manning, for so long criticized as a regular-season stud but a postseason dud, was hoisting the Lombardi Trophy into the damp night air. It was doubly pleasing. He also was named the game's Most Valuable Player, having thrown for 247 yards and one TD.

The Colts had their first world championship since Don McCafferty's bunch defeated Dallas 16-13 in Miami's Orange Bowl to cap the 1970 season.

It was, Manning insisted with a wide grin, a team victory.

"That's been our theme all year; we have won as a team," he said. "Everybody did their part. There was no panic, nobody gave up. We stayed calm the entire game. We truly won this championship as a team and I'm proud to be part of it."

Dungy embraced the moment, and his team.

"This may not be one of our most talented teams but it sure was the one that felt the most love for one another, the most connection," he said. "I love these guys. I know what they went through to win this."

Not This Time

Same venue, same occasion, three years later: Super Bowl XLIV in South Florida.

Different outcome.

Peyton Manning and the Colts set the early tone against the New Orleans Saints, but couldn't close the deal. They led 10-0 in the first quarter and 10-6 at the half, but were overwhelmed in the second en route to a 31-17 loss.

The Colts opened the season with a new head coach—Jim Caldwell succeeded Tony Dungy, who'd retired in January—and 14 consecutive victories. The unbeaten season ended with a 29-17 loss to the New York Jets when Caldwell enraged the fan base by pulling several front-line players in the third quarter. The championship run ended when Saints cornerback and former Indiana University standout Tracy Porter intercepted a Manning pass and returned it 74 yards for a clinching touchdown with just over three minutes remaining.

"There's only one happy team at the end of the season," Caldwell said. "You don't get any trophies for the regular season."

Manning was good, completing 31-of-45 passes for 333 yards with one touchdown and the crippling interception. His Saints counterpart was off the charts. Drew Brees was 32-of-39 for 288 yards and two TDs, and the game's MVP.

Chapter Three

BILL POLIAN

The Fire Continues to Burn Hot

Former Colts president Bill Polian is known for being committed, competitive, passionate, and on occasion, volatile. He has mellowed some, but when Polian got hot under the collar, everyone sweated a little.

During contract negotiations in 1986, one of quarterback Jim Kelly's agents repeatedly disparaged Buffalo's offensive line. Polian, then the Bills' general manager, boiled. He challenged the agent to assume a three-point stance.

"If you know so much about line play, show me how you would deep-set on a defensive end that swims on you," Polian commanded.

Polian once dismissed the Buffalo media with the admonishment, "If you don't like it, get out of town."

When he was asked if Colts coach Jim Mora was on the "hot seat" during an August 2001 interview, Polian got indignant. He shouted the reporter out of his office. Five months later, he fired Mora.

Polian is smart and decisive. He is diligent, gracious, stubborn, innovative, secretive, loyal, prickly, clever, old-fashioned and cutting-edge, quick-witted and quick-tempered.

He has been named the NFL's Executive of the Year five times in voting conducted by *The Sporting News*. The late George Young of the New York Giants is the only other man who has won the award more than three times.

"Any head coach in the league that knows Bill, any assistant coach in the league that knows Bill, would die to work for him," Mora said on the day his hiring was announced in 1998.

Mora's perspective was dramatically different eight months after his firing.

"I won't say anything about him," Mora said tersely. "Nope. Nope. Nothing."

Marv Levy knows Polian as well as any coach in the league. They worked famously together in Buffalo from 1986 through 1992 while Levy was putting his Hall of Fame credentials in order.

"He has a quick fuse, and he has a temper and he gets upset about things," said Levy, who had Polian introduce him at his Hall of Fame induction. "But I've only seen it in defense of the people in his organization."

Polian to the Rescue

Bill Polian's defense mechanism against criticism became patently obvious during the 2001 season, a few weeks after Colts running back Edgerrin James tore the anterior cruciate ligament in his left knee during a game at Kansas City. In the aftermath, before team physicians Arthur Rettig and Tom

Klootwyk made a definitive diagnosis, James practiced briefly once, to test the knee.

That led to a broadside from comedian Jay Mohr, one Polian heard via audiotape, to which he responded with profound indignation during a co-appearance with Mohr on *Mark Patrick on Sports*, WNDE Sports Radio's popular Indianapolis evening drive-time show.

What followed became one of the most talked-about incidents of the Colts' 20 years in Indianapolis.

"First of all," Polian addressed Patrick, "I'd like to read the statement which you played for me on your show at approximately 5:30 yesterday afternoon. This was taken from a tape that you made available to us. This is a transcript of the tape. I'm quoting Mr. Mohr.

"'Jim, I was talking to your boy, Drew Rosenhaus, man. He represents Edgerrin James and told me some wacky things. Turns out, the Edge with his torn ACL, dude, they put him as questionable. They—I'm presuming he means the Colts—'made him practice, put him in a state of denial, the Colts, tore two more ligaments in his knee while practicing with a classic torn ACL. Look for Edgerrin James to get out of Indianapolis quickly. Not a fan of [owner Jim] Irsay.'

"Now I would like to read for you and for anyone else who is interested the transcript of my radio show last night, which ran on your sister station, and I will read it verbatim as I will stand by it.

"'I want to be careful,' this is me speaking, 'I want to be careful about what I say here because I do not have a lawyer in the room and this gentleman I presume will hear from our lawyers shortly. But let me refute this as best I can, categorically almost word by word. "Drew Rosenhaus represents Edgerrin James." Not true to my knowledge. And in order for that to be true, Drew Rosenhaus and Edgerrin James would have had to file a piece of paper and a declaration to that effect with me. And as I said, I was with Edgerrin James Sunday night and he neither filed a paper nor told me about it. So I presume that this is exactly what it is. A lie. I'm going to underline the word lie. This is not a misstatement. This is not a misrepresentation. There are no euphemisms here. This is a lie. L-I-E, pure and simple.'

"Quote Mr. Mohr again.

"'Turns out Edge, with his torn ACL, dude, they put him as questionable.'

"I don't know what he means by that. Perhaps he would be best served to get a translator.

"Quote Mr. Mohr again.

"'They, the Colts, made him practice, put him in a state of denial, the Colts.'

"Again, please translate. I have no idea what that means. I know Edgerrin was not in a state of hypnosis or in a state of panic. I don't know what a state of denial means and I don't know how we put him there. I would categorically say it's untrue, even if I could decipher what it meant.

"Quote Mr. Mohr once again.

"'The Colts tore two more ligaments in his knee while practicing with a classic torn ACL.'

"'I'm not an attorney,' this is me speaking once again, 'but I have a real strong feeling that that statement is subject to legal action. And I will say it's an absolute, complete, total, unadulterated lie. There is not a shred of truth to it. There is not a shred of evidence to back it up. I would challenge Mr. Mohr or anyone else that wants to produce such evidence to do so, and I know they can't because it doesn't exist. And to impugn the integrity of this team, of its doctors, of its administration, is to me absolutely despicable and unconscionable.'"

Coming Up for Air

Finally given a chance to speak, Mohr admitted that he had it wrong, that Rosenhaus was not James's agent:

Jay Mohr: "That was false. That was false. That was absolutely false."

BP: "You told a lie. That was a falsehood, am I correct?"

JM: "That was a falsehood, correct. Drew Rosenhaus does not represent Edgerrin James and I think that...(interrupted)

BP: "Am I correct in that assumption?"

JM: "I've already answered you, Mr. Polian. And that's pretty much..." (interrupted)

BP: "No, you have not answered me. I'm..." (interrupted)

My Turn! No, Mine!

The conversation continued in the same vein:

JM: "OK, can I speak now?"

Mark Patrick: "Go ahead, Jay."

BP: (interrupting) "Answer my question."

MP: "Go ahead, Jay. Mr. Polian, let Jay respond here. Let's see what he says."

BP: "I'd like him to respond to my question!...No euphemisms..." (interrupted)

JM: "No, I'm not telling any jokes, Mr...." (interrupted)

BP: "Respond to the question. He made..." (interrupted)

JM: "Maybe I should call back..." (interrupted)

BP: "He has an obligation to back it up..." (interrupted)

JM: "Maybe we should do this separately if it's not going to be an open conversation."

MP: "All right, Mr. Polian, please."

BP: "I'm not interested in having a conversation with you, sir. I'm interested…" (interrupted)

JM: "Apparently not, because I haven't said anything, Mr. Polian."

BP: "I have no interest in having a conversation with you!"

JM: "Then why are we on the radio right now? Why are you so angry if you're not interested in having a…" (interrupted)

BP: (inaudible)

JM: "You're not letting me speak. Why are you so interested in being on the radio with me if you don't want to have a conversation?"

BP: "I have no desire to have a conversation with you."

JM: "Then hang up."

It Got Worse Before It Got Over

JM: "This guy is crazy. I didn't know you were crazy, Mr. Polian."

BP: "…that Edgerrin tore ligaments in his knee while practicing…" (interrupted)

JM: "I had no idea you were this crazy [talking over inaudible Polian]. No wonder the Colts are in such disarray with someone like you at the helm."

BP: "…and the impunity…" (interrupted)

JM: "[Talking over inaudible Polian] No wonder the Colts are in such disarray with a madman like yourself at the helm of the control."

BP: "…and let him dance around it..." (interrupted)

JM: "You are a madman. This is nuts."

BP: "People's reputations are at stake here."

JM: "Yeah, and your reputation should be very soured on the fact that you let a guy practice with a torn ACL."

BP: "Uh, sir, I'm very happy to deal with that when you deal…" (interrupted)

JM: "Whoa, whoa, whoa. You're happy to deal with what? You're happy to deal with what? You're happy to deal with what? The fact that you let Edgerrin James practice with a torn ACL for three weeks?"

BP: "You have not made…You lied about Drew Rosenhaus. You will not answer me, so I'm going to take it that you're lying." (interrupted, inaudible Polian)

JM: "You're crazy. You're insane. No wonder the Colts are doing so poorly. You are an absolute madman. And everyone listening to the radio knows the general manager of their favorite team is a madman [talking over inaudible Polian]."

Brief silence.

MP: "Mr. Polian, could we…" (interrupted)

JM: "Did you let Edgerrin James practice for three weeks with a torn ACL?"

BP: "Edgerrin James…" (interrupted)

JM: "Yes or no?"

BP: "…did not practice for three weeks! At all! No sir! Absolutely not! Categorically untrue! And you don't have a shred of evidence to back up that statement! Not a shred! That's another lie!" (inaudible)

So it went, until finally, it was over.

Colts fans buzzed about it for weeks. Some supported Polian. Some assailed him. Others were merely amused.

On the Importance of Being "Presidential"

Months later, Bill Polian's concern remained. He felt that (team physicians) Arthur Rettig's and Tom Klootwyk's reputations had been unfairly impugned, that the team and the truth had been assaulted. His ire rose again with the memory.

"Men who are qualified to do their jobs are not to be calumniated by people who have no knowledge or background to question it," he said protectively.

Team president Bill Polian (right) and owner Jim Irsay built the Colts into a perennial contender. (Robert Scheer/The Indianapolis Star)

Jay Mohr was largely uninformed and misinformed. Polian had the high ground, but he lost his temper. What was supposed to be a discussion degenerated into a shouting match, and Polian did most of the shouting.

The show became a spectacle, an embarrassment, and Colts owner Jim Irsay later acknowledged it. He spoke with Polian about the need to conduct himself in a more "presidential" manner.

"When you close the door he understands his shortcomings, and we all have shortcomings. He doesn't shy away from saying, 'I need to straighten that out,'" Irsay said. "Bill has a temper, and it's up to me to point that out. He is a fierce advocate for the Indianapolis Colts."

One to Remember

Player personnel is part science, part art, part instinct, part psychology and an element of informed guesswork. Bill Polian's record is far better than most, but not perfect. He admits his mistakes, and he can laugh about them.

"You bet," he said. "I've made a ton of them."

Like 1991. The Bills had the 26th pick. They had quarterback Brett Favre of Southern Mississippi on their board. Polian, then-Buffalo general manager, loved him. So did owner Ralph Wilson. Coach Marv Levy argued that Buffalo's Jim Kelly was in his prime; the Bills didn't need a quarterback.

So Polian took safety Henry Jones of Illinois. He played 10 years and helped Buffalo to three Super Bowls. But he wasn't Brett Favre. There is only one of those.

"That one sticks in my mind," said Polian, who had plenty of company in bypassing Favre, who was inducted into the Pro Football Hall of Fame in 2016.

Favre went to Atlanta as the 33rd pick and the third quarterback taken in the draft. Dan McGwire and Todd Marinovich went ahead of him.

One to Forget

Many Colts fans have been frustrated by the team's failure to bolster its defense with veteran free agents, but Bill Polian was committed to building through the draft and re-signing his own players.

He plugged in free agents like cornerback Walt Harris on occasion, but he strayed significantly from his policy only in 2001, when he brought in veterans like defensive tackles Mike Wells and Christian Peter and linebacker Mike Morton. Polian hogged the blame when the injury-wracked Colts got little help and went 6-10.

"I think you deserve to be criticized and I hope I'm my own worst critic," he said. "I've preached for years and years that there are no quick fixes. The fact that a guy's a veteran and a name doesn't make him a good player. There has to be a fit. The guy has to have had a track record of success. He still has to have his game.

"We departed from all of those values, if you will, and brought in people who were at the end of their game, that didn't fit. Really, if I look back on it now, Christian Peter was probably the only one that was the right one for this team. Everybody else was just flailing around and that's entirely my fault and we shouldn't have done it."

Contact-Seeking Missile

Bill Polian's father was an Irish immigrant, a meter reader and bookkeeper. His mother was a secretary. Polian learned early that he would get what he wanted only by working for it, and he worked at football.

He wasn't talented enough to play professionally, but his football fervor was A-1. As a high school safety, Polian once came up on the sweep and attacked the ball carrier with such unmitigated violence that he shattered the fibia and the tibia.

His own.

"I was in a cast for 11 months," he recalled.

Salary Cap, a Toothache That Doesn't Quit

Prior to 1993, when the salary cap was implemented, teams had exclusive rights and a franchise could build a team, hold onto it and see it through to maturity. Under that system, the best football people, the most acute talent evaluators, general managers and coaches prospered.

It was pure football: Identify the best players. Sign them. Coach them. Win with them. Keep them. Teams could pay as much as they wanted, but salary costs didn't become prohibitive. Having exclusive rights to players assured that. There was no free agency. There were no bidding wars. Exclusive rights served as a governor on spending.

Clubs like San Francisco, Buffalo and Washington prospered. They built championship-caliber teams and maintained them. So did Dallas, although the Cowboys won the Super Bowl three times in four years through the 1995 season, by which time the salary cap had been in place for three years.

The Cowboys did it by borrowing against their future with gimmicks and back-loaded contracts and voidable years. And when that debt came due, they jettisoned player salaries in a spiral that put them through "cap hell," a run of three successive 5-11 seasons, 2000–02.

That's today's NFL. Each team has the same salary allotment: $80.6 million for 2004. What separates them is the efficiency with which they spend it, how they "manage the cap."

Bill Polian was working in the league office as vice president of football development in 1993. He helped formulate and implement the Collective Bargaining Agreement with which he now contends as president of the Colts. It's a constant irritant.

"What's the salary cap to me? It's an abscessed tooth 365 days a year," said Polian. "However, if we did not have this system, there would be no Indianapolis Colts, no Buffalo Bills, no Carolina Panthers.

"They would not exist, or they would be doormats."

Polian, director of football operations Dom Anile, and their staff had put together a program that placed the Colts in the playoffs four of their first five seasons. The challenge was to maintain and even improve, to continue to contend in an era of unprecedented volatility.

"We have a system that ensures competitive balance and gives cost certainty to the owners," said Polian. "But it mitigates strongly against continuity.

"You hope you can avoid the valleys. I hope you can avoid the tearing-it-down-and-starting-over syndrome. But boy, you'd better draft well and you'd better not have any horrendous breaks along the way."

Colts Got Simpler and Better

When Bill Polian fired coach Jim Mora on January 8, 2002, he did so, he said, because it was his "deeply held conviction" that the Colts needed a new and simpler approach on defense. Mora wouldn't fire Vic Fangio, his defensive coordinator and longtime friend, so Polian fired Mora.

It might not have been necessary had the Colts given Mora and Fangio a draft like the one they executed in 2002: Seven of the club's nine picks were used on defensive players, including end Dwight Freeney, tackle Larry Triplett and linebacker David Thornton.

The Colts did not become a shut-down defense in the Cover-2 scheme new head coach Tony Dungy and defensive coordinator Ron Meeks installed in 2002, but their improvement was substantial.

The Colts yielded 486 points in 2001, the fourth most generous allowance in NFL history, and an average of 30.4 points a game. The numbers were 336 points for a 21-point average in 2003.

The Colts ranked 29th in total defense in 2001, permitting 357.2 yards a game. The 2003 number was 299.3 yards, the ranking No. 11.

Polian Gets His Man

With the 29th pick in the 2004 NFL draft, the Colts weren't likely to get a run-smothering defensive tackle or game-changing linebacker. They weren't likely to get anyone better than they already had at those positions, and they knew it. The man they determined they wanted, and were likely to be able to get, was Iowa safety Bob Sanders.

Sanders was a three-time first-team All-Big Ten honoree, but he stood only 5'8", a circumstance that worked against his early selection. Moreover, as a senior he had missed three games with a stress fracture in his right foot and played nine others with a pin holding the bone together.

So when the Colts got offers, they twice traded down, from 29th to 44th, where they took Sanders, a hitter with big-play aptitude.

Sanders has yet to prove that he can handle an NFL tight end who is 10 inches taller and 60 pounds heavier. That he can win a red-zone jump ball with a 6'3" receiver. That he can he cover the fade. And that pairing him on the back line with second-year man Mike Doss, who is 5'10", won't provide a vulnerability opponents will exploit.

But his selection is reminiscent of another year, another player, another time Bill Polian opted for the unconventional, and won.

It was 1988, and the Buffalo Bills didn't have a first-round pick. Polian had his eye on an Oklahoma State running back, but his prospect was coming off knee surgery and there were concerns about its efficacy.

Polian acquired videotape of the surgery. He showed it to the Bills' team doctor. He grilled him on the procedure.

Satisfied, he played his informed hunch with the 40th pick. Thurman Thomas played 13 seasons and rushed for 12,074 yards.

Injuries that cost them draft position aren't the only link that Sanders and Thomas share. Both were asleep when Polian called to inform them they had been chosen. Sanders dozed off in a recliner amidst a gathering of about 50 at his parents' Erie, Pennsylvania, home.

The similarity was not lost on Polian, who could only chuckle.

Bill Polian was among the NFL's best at assessing and acquiring talent. (Matt Kryger/*The Indianapolis Star*)

"Similar ability at a different position," he said. "Please God, [Sanders] turns out as well."

Establishing Priorities and Meeting Them

The late Paul Brown is one of the many luminaries with whom Bill Polian worked on the NFL's elite competition committee.

"There are two things you need to compete in this league," the old Cleveland coach and owner once counseled Polian. "A quarterback and a pass rusher."

Polian used his first draft pick as president of the Colts—No. 1 overall in the 1998 draft—to fill the former position with Peyton Manning. Polian took running back Edgerrin James with the fourth pick in 1999, when he also picked up some pass rush help in unrestricted free agent end Chad Bratzke.

The centerpiece pass rusher was the target the next time the Colts ventured anywhere near the top of the draft—the 11th selection in 2002. Polian grabbed end Dwight Freeney.

Manning went to the Pro Bowl 14 times, was a five-time league MVP, a two-time Super Bowl winner, and a Super Bowl MVP. James? He led the NFL in rushing in 1999 and 2000 and went to four Pro Bowls.

Irish Eyes Were Smiling

Bill Polian is an Irishman and proud of it, and he once expressed that pride in a manner that surprised Marv Levy.

"In our earlier days, we were at a piano bar once and they were singing Irish songs," Levy recalled of his time as Buffalo head coach. "Bill got to the mike and he knocked them out. He can sing."

Rebuilding… Without Polian

One of the most decorated executives in NFL history saw his association with the Colts end shortly after the team finished the 2011 season with a 2-14 record. Polian was fired by owner Jim Irsay. The end came despite Polian's stunning 14-year resume with the Colts: 11 playoff appearances, two trips to the Super Bowl, one world championship.

Irsay described it as an "intuitive decision… Clearly we are in a rebuilding stage."

Executive Orders

Polian's departure from the Colts shortly after the 2011 season set a chain of events in motion that led to a flurry of individual accolades that firmly established him as one of the most accomplished front-office executives in NFL history.

He was included in the Buffalo Bills' Wall of Fame in 2012 and added to the Colts' Ring of Honor in 2017.

In between was the greatest individual honor of all: enshrinement in the Pro Football Hall of Fame as a member of the Class of 2015.

"I owe it all to the players and coaches," Polian said during his acceptance speech. "That's why I'm here, because of what they did."

Among those in attendance at Polian's enshrinement were quarterbacks Peyton Manning, Polian's first pick as GM of the Colts in 1998, and Jim Kelly, the triggerman for Polian's high-powered offenses in Buffalo. He was presented by long-time Bills coach and friend Marv Levy, himself a member of the Pro Football Hall of Fame.

"Everything I have, everything that's good that has come to me in this business is because of him," Polian said of Levy. "Everything I know about pro football I learned from him, and most of the things I know about life I've learned from him.

"The biggest thrill tonight is to be able to share it with my family, and to have Jim Kelly and Peyton Manning here, too, because they're the reason I'm here."

Polian closed by quoting New York Yankees legend Lou Gehrig.

"Today, I am the luckiest man on the face of the earth," he said.

Chapter Four

PEYTON MANNING

No Music for This "Line" Dance

Let's deal with this up front, since it is the aspect of quarterback Peyton Manning's play that attracts the most attention and is the matter about which he has become the most sensitive.

We're talking about his pre-snap "activity." It has become Manning's signature, his trademark, the salient characteristic of the style and efficiency with which he plays the game.

Manning typically breaks the huddle and approaches the line of scrimmage with about 18 seconds remaining on the play clock, a little more if the Colts go with the no-huddle offense they used so extensively in 2003.

He needs the time.

He studies the defense. He points and gestures. He signals and shouts. He dances up and down the line. Manning becomes an aerobics instructor, a drum major, a disco dancer, a one-man fire drill. His calisthenics continue as the play clock ticks toward zero and the muttering in the stands reaches full roar.

Defenses don't like it. Television analysts rail about it. Crowds boil at road games, and the catcalls are audible even at home: "Shut up and quit jumping around. Just run the damn play."

After losses, they sometimes still echo on Mondays, on Indianapolis talk radio.

"'I'll tell you what the problem is: Peyton takes too much time at the line. They can't get any rhythm,'" one caller will say.

Or, "'How do we know if it's Tom Moore's fault if Peyton's always changing the play?'"

It's curious that one of the league's most productive offenses would be anyone's "fault," but there is a very straightforward explanation.

"This is what our offense is. This is Tom Moore's offense," said Manning. "I think we've grown through the years, but this is not me out there just making things up and doing them. This is what the offense is."

Manning might be the manic marionette we see each Sunday, but if he were to go down with an injury, his backup would dance the same dance. Offensive coordinator Tom Moore would reduce the reads and options somewhat, but the quarterback's role wouldn't change.

"It's something that people are going to talk about because it's different," said former Colts' coach Tony Dungy. "We do something different than most people."

No team makes as many adjustments at the line as the Colts do, although some of the time all the jumping and gesticulating signifies nothing. There are dummy calls. It's the defense's job to sort it all out.

The Colts' offensive scheme required quarterback Peyton Manning and center Jeff Saturday to make adjustments prior to the snap of the ball. (Robert Scheer/**The Indianapolis Star**)

In NFL parlance, the Colts' attack is called a "check-with-me" offense. No other quarterback is as busy, but Manning isn't out there calling audibles every snap. Moore typically sends in two or three plays. Manning's job is to determine the defense's front, coverage and intent, then check to the option best suited to attacking it.

"One of them should work," said Moore, a 40-year coaching veteran with 26 years of NFL experience, 16 as coordinator.

When Manning Talks, Opponents Listen

Quarterback Peyton Manning might be a bit self-conscious about his pre-snap gyrations, but opponents hold his ability to read defenses and adapt at the line of scrimmage in high esteem.

"Every defense has a weakness," said Browns defensive coordinator Dave Campo. "Every front has a weakness. Every coverage has a weakness. If you have a guy who has a good feel for where you're sitting and can get you into a better play, more power to him. That does hurt the defense."

Manning has that acuity. It is precisely what was required by Tom Moore's system.

"He's the best we've come across at it," said Tennessee coach Jeff Fisher.

"Nobody does it better," said Detroit coach Steve Mariucci. "He just stands there and tries to get you to show your defense."

Football is a chess match. The idea is to get an edge, however small. Of course it doesn't always work. There are fits and spurts. And defenses counter. They shift, disguise, tease. The play clock frequently reaches three seconds, two seconds, even one, before the football is snapped.

"You'd like to be quicker," said Moore, who is in his seventh year with the Colts, "but you have to do what you have to do."

Sometimes that's a true audible, although Dungy estimates the Colts average only four or five a game.

"We communicate all week about, 'Hey, if we get this front with this linebacker shifted over, we're going to check and go somewhere else,'" said center Jeff Saturday. "It's not like we have our entire playbook every time we go to the line of scrimmage.

"Most of the time people think we're audibling, we're not. Those are plays we go to the line with."

Big Money, but a Deal to Live With

The seven-year, $98 million contract Peyton Manning signed in March 2004 made him the best-paid player in NFL history and guaranteed him $34.5 million, his two-installment signing bonus. It also virtually guaranteed something else he held dear.

"I'm glad to be a Colt for life," said Manning. "This is where I live. This is where I built my home. I'm looking forward to being here for a long, long time and playing for the Colts and for Tony [Dungy] and for Bill [Polian] and for Jim [Irsay]."

Manning's annual average—$14 million—was unprecedented. So is the signing bonus, which nearly doubled the next largest ever awarded, $20 million to Philadelphia quarterback Donovan McNabb in 2002.

But the huge numbers would be kind to the Colts, at least for the next four seasons.

Take a Moment, Be Nice

It was a Tuesday, the standard NFL players' day off, but as the AFC's No. 2 seed in the 1999 playoffs, the Colts had an open week and coach Jim Mora had given his team an extra day.

So Peyton Manning was at the airport, looking forward to a brief visit home to New Orleans. He had a book in hand, *The Junction Boys*, the story of Bear Bryant's days at Texas A&M, and Manning thought he had a little time to read it.

No such luck. Manning's flight was delayed 30 minutes. He obliged 30 autograph seekers. He read zero pages.

"Basically, you're an open target," shrugged Manning. "You're fair game."

So he smiled and he signed.

There really are only a couple of places Manning would hope not to be hassled—places like the doctor's office and church, but even there, people approach, incapable of resisting the urge to connect with celebrity.

A fan once intruded in the doctor's waiting room. Would Peyton take just a moment to sign his X-rays? Another time, in church, at benediction, Manning felt a poke. One of the faithful offered a jersey and a pen; he had come, apparently, to worship God and Peyton.

Both times, Manning signed.

"I learned from my dad," he said. "It takes five seconds to smile and be nice. It takes the same amount of time to be a jerk. So smile and be nice."

That philosophy is a product of Manning's nature and nurture. He is the son of a courtly southern gentleman. He is, himself, a courtly southern gentleman. That, as much as his Hall of Famer in waiting–caliber play, stamps him and makes him the NFL icon he has become.

"Peyton has always tried to please," said his father, Archie, a Mississippi native who resides in New Orleans. "He's always tried to do what's right. He's always enjoyed people and he really treasures his friends."

Cost of Business Is Rising

Peyton Manning had a lot to treasure in his $98 million contract and the accompanying $34.5 million signing bonus in March 2004. The agreement raised the standard for a franchise quarterback's compensation. It also raised some eyebrows.

"Yeah," said former Seattle coach Mike Holmgren, "the bar has kind of been set."

"Yes, it absolutely gives me pause," said Atlanta owner Arthur Blank, who dealt with the ripple effect when it came time to sign Falcons quarterback Michael Vick to his second contract. "Sometimes it stops me in my tracks.... Sometimes I wake up at night."

Just for Starters...

The Colts aren't the only ones who invested in Peyton Manning's career. He paid some dues of his own as a rookie.

Manning lost a total of 11 games in high school and college. He lost 13 as the Colts' rookie starting quarterback in 1998. He was forewarned.

"My dad told me before the draft," Peyton recalled, "'This is going to be tough. You're going to be the No. 1 pick and you're going to a bad team. That's how it works.'"

Manning's second season was different. The Colts went 13-3. They won 11 straight during one stretch, three more than his dad, Archie, won in any of his 14 NFL seasons with New Orleans, Houston and Minnesota.

Taking His Lumps, and Breaking Through

In 1998 Peyton Manning joined George Shaw (1955), Bert Jones (1973), Mike Pagel (1982) and Jeff George (1990) as the only rookie quarterbacks in Colts history to start on opening day. He passed for 302 yards and a touchdown. He also threw three interceptions. The Colts lost 24-15 to Miami.

"He's got a great attitude, so he's going to be fine," offered Dolphins quarterback Dan Marino, who helped convert two of those interceptions into touchdowns. "He's going to be a great player in this league; I believe that."

Game two figured to be better. Manning threw three more interceptions and lost a fumble at the Colts' two-yard line against New England's shifting, blitzing defense. Four turnovers became 20 Patriots points and a 29-6 loss.

Two starts, seven turnovers converted into 34 points.

"We were playing mind games with him," said New England cornerback Ty Law. "It's all part of growing up.

He's not going to get the respect of [Denver quarterback John] Elway or Marino until he beats a couple of guys."

Coach Jim Mora offered no respite. He kept sending his prize rookie into the maelstrom.

Validation came in game seven, at San Francisco. Manning read the defense and felt the rush. He managed the game. He threw for 231 yards and three touchdowns with no interceptions. The Colts weren't finished losing and Manning would continue to make mistakes, but he arrived that Sunday at 3Com Park.

Like Marino, 49ers quarterback Steve Young saluted Manning's attitude.

"The jump from college to the pros is like going from a tricycle to a car on the highway," said Young. "It's the speed. When I first started playing, I swore there were 30 guys on defense and the field was too small.

"The important thing is you have a good frame of mind about it, that you're going to take some hits, physically and mentally. He seems like the kind of guy that has the mental attributes to pull it off."

Manning's mental attributes have proven his greatest strength, but he deemed it all empty praise after a couple of immensely controversial officials' calls and some Young magic rendered a 21-0 Colts lead a 34-31 San Francisco victory.

"Moral victories, even those that exist in this league, really shouldn't," said Manning. "You try to take something from every game, but this one probably hurt the worst of them all season. The game slipped out from under us."

For the Record, and There Have Been a Few

Peyton Manning threw 28 interceptions but set NFL rookie records for completions (326), attempts (575), yards (3,739), touchdowns (26) and consecutive games with a touchdown pass (13) in 1998.

Good as those numbers were, they pale in comparison to his statistics in 2003, when Manning was voted to the Pro Bowl for the fourth time in five years and shared the league's Most Valuable Player Award with Tennessee quarterback Steve McNair.

Manning led the NFL in completions (379) and completion percentage (67.0) while finishing second in attempts (566), interception percentage (1.8) and passer rating (99.0).

Tony Dungy, who succeeded Jim Mora as Colts head coach after the 2001 season, had the benefit of perspective. He can survey Manning's first six seasons, and he saw Manning's rugged rookie season and the huge contract he was awarded in March 2004 as investments in a career that still has tremendous upside.

"I guess as a quarterback you're always viewed by championships. That's what defines people," Dungy conceded. "But Peyton has played as well as anybody coming into the league. That's what I think people kind of lose track of.

"I played with Joe Montana when he was a rookie, and he got 15 snaps in the whole season and didn't really start playing until his third year. And most of your high-drafted quarterbacks don't play right away. Steve McNair, I thought they did a great job bringing him along. But he didn't get to play those first three or four years.

"Peyton learned from his mistakes and learned by doing and put up some numbers that most guys are putting up

*Quarterback Peyton Manning was named the league's Most Valuable Player five times. (Matt Detrich/*The Indianapolis Star*)*

during their second five years in the league. What he's done in the context of league history is just phenomenal. He's got probably, if he wants to, 12 to 15 years left to play."

Playoff Futility a Heavy Burden

Only one quarterback in NFL history threw for more than 4,000 yards in six successive seasons. His name is Peyton Manning.

Only one player reached 25,000 passing yards faster than Manning, who threw for 24,885 yards through 96 games and six seasons. His name is Dan Marino.

Since coming into the NFL in 1998, Manning threw for more yards and more touchdowns (167) in his first six seasons than any other quarterback.

It's an enviable track record, but one that played to a weary refrain, at least until January 2004: "Yeah, but he's 0-3 in the playoffs."

Manning heard it. How could he not?

"A lot of times it's the Colts have been to the playoffs three times, but ol' Peyton, he's 0-3 in the playoffs," said Manning.

"It's not always fair," former Denver coach Mike Shanahan said, but "everybody is always evaluated by playoff games. That's just the nature of the system."

Still, Manning bore an inordinate share of the burden of blame. The Colts' defense and running game were substandard.

Yielding an average of 211.7 rushing yards while running for only 76.3 yards is a simple equation. It adds up to 0-3, a 19-16 loss to Tennessee in a 1999 AFC divisional round game, a 23-17 overtime loss at Miami in 2000 and a 41-0 splattering at the New York Jets in 2002.

Still, Manning's numbers were unbecoming a four-time Pro Bowl player: 50 completions in 105 pass attempts (.476) for 558 yards and a single touchdown with two interceptions. His completion percentage was miles off his .629 career number. His 59.1 passer rating was almost 30 points lower than his career rating and a tick short of a full 40 off the 99.0 he posted during the 2003 season.

A Memorable Breakthrough

Anyone seeking the Colts' pressure point going into the 2003 playoffs needed look no further than No. 18. The man under center was under the gun.

He came out firing. Peyton Manning completed 44 of 56 passes (.786) for 681 yards and eight touchdowns with zero interceptions as the Colts beat Denver, 41-10, and Kansas City, 38-31. His quarterback rating was 156.9, a tick off the "perfect rating," 158.3.

It might have been the greatest two-game playoff run by any quarterback ever.

And it ended the next week, during a 24-14 loss at New England in the AFC championship game. Under pressure with his receivers unable to get open, Manning was 23 for 47 for 237 yards and one touchdown with four interceptions. His rating was 35.5, the third worst of his career.

It's a tough game, a tough league. Manning looked jittery, panicked, lost, a lot like he did during the 41-0 wild card loss at New York that excused the Colts from the 2002 playoffs. As disappointing as it was, there was nothing to do but learn from it, do it better next time, and Manning has proved resilient and tough enough to do that.

This is a player who in six years has been out once because of injury, that a broken jaw suffered against Miami in 2001. He was back after a single snap on the sidelines. He will not permit a loss to brand him.

"I have a definition of myself and the things that I know I can do," said Manning. "But there are so many different people that are going to have definitions of you, and so many people that are going to say he's this or he's that.

"I can't control what everybody else says or thinks. I certainly would like to win a Super Bowl, and more than one. I've played six years and I haven't done that yet. I've been close, and I'm going to keep sawing wood and keep trying to get there."

Football Cum Laude

Peyton Manning is bright. He graduated cum laude from Tennessee with a 3.6 grade point average in speech communications—in only three years.

He played four years in a sophisticated offense with the Volunteers, and he grew up in the game.

His father, Archie, was the No. 2 pick in the 1971 NFL draft and the 1978 NFC Most Valuable Player. He played 14 NFL seasons. Peyton's older brother, Cooper, played wide receiver at Mississippi until a congenital spinal condition forced him to give up the game. Younger brother Eli played quarterback at Ole Miss, just like Archie, and was made the first pick of the 2004 NFL draft by San Diego, which then traded him to the New York Giants.

So when Peyton got to the Colts in 1998, he considered himself well-versed, even accomplished, ready for whatever complexities coordinator Tom Moore's offense might pose.

The Colts wasted no time immersing him. On draft day, they presented him with him a two-inch-thick playbook. Manning was undaunted. The tome appeared no more imposing than Tennessee's, and he said so.

"They told me, 'That's only about a quarter of it,'" Manning said. "I was feeling pretty good, and they humbled me quickly."

Turkey and Dressing, Friends and Videotape

The playbook Peyton Manning received from the Colts on draft day in 1998 posed no problem. Excellence tolerates no shortcuts, and no one prepares harder, better, than Manning. That was the case his rookie year, and he continues to prepare with singular diligence. That's why he shut off the video machine well after midnight Thanksgiving night, 2003.

Colts practice had ended early, at 1:30, to give the players and coaches a chance to get home to be with their families. Manning brought defensive lineman Brad Scioli, guard Rick DeMulling and a couple other bachelor teammates home to his wife, Ashley.

She cooked up a spread and the players dug in. After his teammates left, Manning took a nap, then watched Eli play quarterback for Ole Miss against Mississippi State.

At game's end, Peyton retired to the "bat cave," his in-house video room. It took him an hour to review the day's practice film. Forward. Back. Rewind. Review. Forward.

Back. Rewind. Review. How's the fake? How's the drop-back? Where are the feet? The ball position? The follow-through? Threw to the right, to Marvin Harrison. OK. Back. What if I had worked Reggie Wayne? What was he doing with his route? He's open. What if I'd gone there?

And always, always scrutinizing his own technique.

"The older you get, the more your mechanics fall apart," said Manning. "You stop faking as well. You drop the ball a little bit. You lose your discipline. Those things happen easily during a game, too. You start out hot, then maybe in the third or fourth quarter, you don't finish a throw quite as much."

Three days later, Manning threw four touchdown passes against a New England defense that had permitted six in its first 11 games, a defense that would help the Patriots win the Super Bowl for the second time in three years.

Noteworthy Effort

Peyton Manning's penchant for preparation is legendary, but occasionally it surprises.

Colts vice president of public relations Craig Kelley gave the same orientation speech he always does when Manning was a rookie in 1998. Kelley explained that the players represented the Colts, that there were certain expectations and dos and don'ts in dealing with the media, and so on.

Kelley looked up. He looked at Manning. The quarterback was taking notes.

Manning Is the "1"

It was a slow afternoon in the Colts' locker room and Peyton Manning was in one of those Regis Philbin moods.

For something less than a million dollars, who could name the 20 quarterbacks who have spent time on the roster with him since his arrival in 1998? The reward wouldn't approach a million dollars. The only thing at stake was bragging rights over Manning.

"Brock Huard, Kelly Holcomb, Mark Rypien, Steve Walsh, Billy Joe Hobert, Cory Sauter, Jim Druckenmiller."

"That's seven," Manning said, smiling.

A deep breath.

"Stoney Case, James MacPherson, Tom Arth, Greg Zolman, Jim Kubiak, Bill Musgrave … Pete Gonzalez … Roderick Robinson."

"That's 15," Manning said. "Give up?"

"Not yet. Can I use a lifeline?"

"You don't have one."

Oh.

"Mike Quinn."

"That's 16."

"Gus Ornstein."

"That's 17."

"I know, Gino Torretta."

"That was before I got here," Manning said.

Finally, after a long pause, the white flag was waved.

"I give up."

That made Manning's day.

"Doug Nussmeier, Mark Hartsell and Dave Meyer," he said, completing the list.

The difficulty in recalling Manning's long list of understudies was understandable. Several were here today, gone before the end of training camp. Druckenmiller, a former first-round pick of the San Francisco 49ers, was signed in January 2003 and never made it to camp.

Such is the lifespan of a Colts quarterback not named Manning.

Holcomb worked alongside Manning for three years, two as his backup. But Manning's durability and productivity kept Holcomb and so many of his QB colleagues inactive on game day. Holcomb never took a snap from center during the regular season. The only ones who have are Walsh (21 snaps in 1999), Rypien (22 in '01) and Huard (22 in '03).

"You understand that," Holcomb said. "This is his team."

In his first six seasons, Manning had missed only one play because of injury. That occurred in 2001 against Miami when Manning suffered a fractured jaw on a hit by Dolphins defensive lineman Lorenzo Bromell.

He wobbled to the sideline, bloodied but hardly broken. He quickly located his senses and returned to the game.

"Even though you're a backup, you're still involved in it and you're only one play away," said Huard. "A couple of years ago Peyton broke his jaw and all of a sudden Ryp had to go in there. You've got to be ready for that moment.

"You're practicing. You're doing everything. You're just not getting those 70 snaps on Sunday."

Playing for Keeps

No Colt was more competitive than Peyton Manning, and it's easy to see why. He grew up around sports, in the New Orleans Saints locker room tagging after his father Archie, at older brother Cooper's games, and on the field and court competing with Cooper.

"We used to play basketball, one-on-one, to see who took out the garbage," recalled Cooper, two years Peyton's senior. "When it was 18-18 and the next point won, somebody was going to get a forearm to the head. The games never ended."

Maximizing Efficiency and Minimizing Mistakes

For all the achievement of his first six seasons, Peyton Manning was still striving, still improving. He knew his strengths and weaknesses. He knew his numbers. He knew he pitched 23 interceptions in 2001 and 19 in 2002.

That didn't prevent head coach Tony Dungy from pointing it out. He provided a detailed accounting of each one: down and distance, time, score, game situation.

The idea is to not throw one on third and 11 from your opponent's 20-yard line during the third quarter of a close game. Take the field goal. Get something. Force the issue, throw into coverage, only when it's warranted, when circumstances are desperate.

Only one quarterback threw more interceptions than Manning's 19 in 2002; Minnesota's Daunte Culpepper had 23. Only one threw more than Manning's 23 in 2001; Kansas City's Trent Green had 24.

Of course the Colts ran a high-risk offense and only a handful of quarterbacks attempted more passes than Manning, who threw 591 in 2002 and 547 the year before. His interception total for those two seasons (41) was a third more than that of the NFL's gold standard at his position.

Green Bay's Brett Favre, who is not a bashful passer, threw 31.

"Part of me still wants to defend the four years before [Dungy] got here," said Manning. "I was dying at times making those aggressive throws, but that's how we were living, too. We weren't scoring by throwing short passes."

Offensive coordinator Tom Moore instilled an aggressive attitude in his young quarterback.

"No guts, no blue chips," was Moore's oft-repeated refrain.

Tuesdays are the players' day off, but the Colts are invited to join the coaches for a voluntary game-planning session. Manning was a regular attendee. He recalls walking into the meeting room many weeks during his first four seasons with the Colts and seeing the dry-erase board covered with way-deep pass routes.

"I'd think, 'I may need to hit a cutoff man to get the ball to that guy,'" recalled Manning. "There would be 40-, 50-yard throwback, bomb throws, aggressive, down-the-field throws.

"That's how we were winning. Our defense was not great. We were living by that. You take chances. You're aggressive with your throws. You just get that mentality."

Manning is the coachable superstar. He took Dungy's counsel to heart. Manning remained aggressive when circumstances dictated, but threw a career-low 10 interceptions in 2003 while completing a club-record 67.0 percent of his passes for a league-leading 4,267 yards and 29 touchdowns.

Seeing Is the Best Preparation for Doing

"Visualization" is one of the many skills sports psychologists stress, and among the most important. Peyton Manning employs it extensively and effectively, and he developed the capacity entirely on his own.

It derives from his father's legendary All-American career at Ole Miss, 1968–70. There are few videotapes of Archie Manning's games, but the family has an extensive collection of audiotapes, and Peyton began listening to them when he was a kid.

He would put in a tape of the radio broadcast, pull on the headphones, and see the plays in his mind's eye while he listened.

He still does it, but the quarterback he sees wears No. 18. It's him.

"I call it 'playing the game in my mind,'" said Peyton. "I'll try to play the game in my mind. When I'm watching film, I try to picture what it's going to look like. You picture good things, but bad things pop in there. You picture yourself throwing an interception.

"I think it helps me; when the game comes, I'm not surprised. I've been there before."

Routine Excellence Follows a Script

It's nine a.m. game day, four hours before kickoff, but already, Peyton Manning is in the house. No one is more diligent in preparation. No one is more slave to routine.

Manning's manner is purposeful, but unhurried. He pulls on sweatpants, a T-shirt, turf shoes, a cap. By 9:30, he's in the RCA Dome training room. Head trainer Hunter Smith is taping Manning's ankles. Manning is reading the game program. He concentrates on the "Colts Connections" section, in which any ties to the opponents are listed.

"We'll find something that's left out or something in there about some assistant scout who played basketball in Ohio, therefore that's with the Bengals game or whatever," said Manning.

It's 10 a.m. Smith gives Manning an arm-and-shoulder rubdown. The chatter focuses on college football, usually Manning's Tennessee Volunteers or Smith's Florida State Seminoles. At 10:10, Manning organizes his locker, checks his pads and visits with his teammates.

Fifty minutes later, he is out on the field, chatting with acquaintances on the opposing team. Business begins at 11:15. That's when Manning and his receivers start "pre-pregame," a pitch-and-catch session that takes the quarterback and his receivers through the entire route tree. Ins. Outs. Slants. Curls. Short. Intermediate. Long.

"It's not superstitious to where if you go out at 11 instead of 11:05 you're going to lose," said Manning. "You just try to keep a routine. You know how long everything takes."

Routine provides order, clarity, calm. Routine is rhythm. Rhythm is football.

It's 11:45. Back in the locker room. Manning pulls on his knee brace, his pads and uniform. There's time to cover a point or two in the game plan with a teammate.

Then it's team warmups. They begin at 12:20. Or 12:21. Depends on whether kickoff is 1:07 or 1:08. Manning isn't the only one addicted to routine.

"It's just the amount [of time] it takes to warm up," explained head coach Tony Dungy. "And then there's 14 minutes in the locker room after warmups."

Dress Rehearsal

Peyton Manning has improved, and his marriage to the former Ashley Thompson was a boon, but he remains better at matching a play call to a defense than a shirt to a pair of pants. Paisley and plaid are not priorities. He used to consult photos of shirts, slacks and ties arranged in complementary combinations by his mother, Olivia.

It's not Manning's favorite subject, but it helps that Terry Bradshaw has similar difficulties. Bradshaw won four Super Bowl titles with the Pittsburgh Steelers. He looks absolutely dapper on Fox Television's NFL studio show, but he admitted to Manning a few years ago that he facilitates coordination by numbering his clothes.

When word of that got out, Manning was confronted on a road trip by a sportswriter asking if he had dressed by the numbers that morning.

Manning studied his interrogator.

"This guy needs a few Polaroids of his own," he thought. Ever polite and obliging, Manning said nothing.

Can Talk a Good Game, Too

Peyton Manning's poise extends well beyond the field. He is comfortable and equipped to deal with almost any situation. In that regard, he is a chip off the old block. His father, Archie, is the embodiment of southern grace, and after a legendary Ole Miss career and 14 years in the NFL, Archie embarked on a successful speaking career.

He gives only about 40 speeches a year now, but at one point did 80 or 90 annually and could have doubled that number had he been so inclined, and they are lucrative. He earns $15,000 to $20,000 for a keynote-type address.

Peyton does about a half dozen but seldom makes a commitment during the season, at better than double the fee. "He's $35,000 or $40,000," said Archie, who does a couple engagements a year with Peyton. "He's a lot more expensive than I am."

Gone, Never Forgotten

When the time comes for Peyton Manning to be inducted into the Pro Football Hall of Fame, the freshest memories and his most recent exploits undoubtedly will resonate from his time with the Denver Broncos.

Yet such a large part of his resume, even his essence, will be tied to his 14 seasons with the Colts. They selected him with the first overall pick in the 1998 draft. He rewarded their decision with extended excellence before the team released him following the 2011 season and he signed with the Broncos.

At the time of his departure from Indianapolis, Manning was the NFL's only four-time Most Valuable Player. He led the franchise into the playoffs in 11 of his first 13 seasons, including nine straight that tied an NFL record. He was MVP of Super Bowl XLI, when the Colts defeated the Chicago Bears, and the starter for Super Bowl XLIV, when they lost to the New Orleans Saints.

Owner Jim Irsay was emotional and exalting in March 2012 when he announced the team's decision to release Manning. "In the history of sports through the last century," he said, "there's been in team sports a handful of Hall of Fame-great players that have done incredible things for franchises. I know (Manning) parallels the handful of people through time that has meant so much to the franchise.

"I know in my heart and in the hearts of fans, it's unparalleled for the Colts. It's a difficult day here of shared pain between Peyton, myself, the fans, everyone . . . the 18 jersey will never be worn again by a Colt on the field.

"There will be no other Peyton Manning."

Manning exchanged hugs with Irsay. He talked of being a Colt for most of his adult life, of building and sharing lasting friendships. He was about to leave Indianapolis, but Manning insisted, "I'll always be a Colt. That will never change.

"This is a relationship business with coaches, teammates, support staff," he added, his voice cracking. "The Colts have the greatest equipment guys in the world. I think about those type of relationships. Not necessarily always on the field and the touchdown throw to win the game. It's behind the scenes, the laughs, the stories, the time spent together. Those are the memories and those aren't going away. Those will be with me for the rest of my life. There are so many. I certainly can't pick one. I just know I've been very fortunate, very blessed. I'm truly appreciative and thankful."

From Indy to Denver to Canton

Four years to the day after an emotional departure from the Colts, Manning once again found himself at odds with his emotions.

It was March 7, 2016, and it was time. After 18 seasons, four trips to the Super Bowl, two world championships, a record five MVP awards and a slew of all-time and single-season records, Manning announced his retirement.

Occasionally he had to pause and compose himself.

"Life is not shrinking for me. It's morphing into a whole new world of possibilities," he said in Denver, his post-Indianapolis NFL residence for four years. "There's a scripture reading, 2 Timothy 4:7: I have fought the good fight and I have finished the race. I have kept the faith.

"Well I have fought the good fight. I've finished my football race and after 18 years, it's time. God bless all of you and God bless football."

No longer would teams find themselves in a stare-down at the line of scrimmage with Manning, his arms flapping and his head wagging back and forth as he analyzed the defense and audibled to a better play.

Manning was finished, but only after setting all-time NFL records with 71,940 passing yards and 539 touchdowns. He also set single-season marks in 2013 with 5,477 yards and 55 touchdowns. He's the league's only five-time MVP and the only quarterback to lead two teams—the Broncos in 2015 and the Colts in 2006—to Super Bowl championships.

Shortly after saying his goodbyes in Denver, Manning returned to his first NFL home—Indianapolis—for another memorable ceremony. Owner Jim Irsay announced the Colts were retiring Manning's No. 18 and beginning construction of a statue of Manning that will rest outside of Lucas Oil Stadium.

"Actions are the most powerful things in life, more powerful than words," Irsay said.

Manning was touched.

"I can't tell you how special this news is to me," he said.

Manning spent several minutes recounting his 14 seasons with the Colts. He rehashed major moments on the field and thanked former teammates, coaches, front-office individuals and the franchise's support staff.

"It's always important to me to be a good teammate and to have the respect of your teammates and the coaches you played for," he said. "Also, if you can have the respect of the players you played against and the coaches you played against."

Manning then was asked about his possible place in NFL history.

"It's certainly nice and humbling when you hear your name mentioned in the conversation," he said. "It's nice and humbling."

More accolades await. During the 2017 season, the Colts will unveil Manning's statue on the north plaza outside of Lucas Oil Stadium, his No. 18 jersey will be officially retired and he will become the fourteenth inductee to the Ring of Honor. Finally, Manning is a lock to be a first-ballot addition to the Pro Football Hall of Fame in Canton, Ohio.

He's eligible to be considered for the Class of 2021.

In a declaration honoring Manning, Irsay ended by noting "the conclusion of Peyton Manning's playing career has caused us to reflect fondly on his epic journey and to conclude that the likes of him will never be seen again."

Chapter Five

MARVIN HARRISON

It's Marvin Time

Tie ballgame. The clock reads 0:30. The air over Pro Player Stadium is thick with tension. The sellout crowd of 74,096 is rapt, breathless. The Miami defensive huddle is tightly focused. The Dolphins know what they must do.

"Stop 88," said Sam Madison, Miami's Pro Bowl cornerback, who 30 minutes later would rue, "We didn't."

No. 88 is the Indianapolis Colts' go-to guy, wide receiver Marvin Harrison, and the Colts went to him.

At the Colts 32-yard line, Harrison lined up on the right side, broke downfield, then cut sharply over the middle. Quarterback Peyton Manning hit him for 16 yards.

At the Colts 48, Harrison set wide, right, again. Another crossing route. Another strike. Another 18 yards.

After a one-yard loss by running back Edgerrin James, Mike Vanderjagt kicked a 53-yard field goal for a 37-34 victory on the game's final play.

"If it works, keep running it. It was the same play both times," said Harrison, who caught eight passes for 125 yards that December day in 1999.

Harrison kept working, and the Colts kept going to him, 1,102 times, for 14,580 yards and 128 touchdowns, all franchise records. The wonder of it is that he continued to get open—wide open—time after time for 13 splendid seasons.

Running a Route to Canton

No one had caught more passes through the first eight seasons of a career than Marvin Harrison. Not Jerry Rice. Not Sterling Sharpe. Not Herman Moore or Keyshawn Johnson. No one.

For his whole career, when Harrison set up wide and broke into his pass route, he ran a career path that took him to Canton, Ohio, and the Pro Football Hall of Fame.

He was the second person in his family to arrive.

"I never even thought about me going," said Harrison, "so I never thought about my mother beating me. For her to be there, that's quite an honor."

Linda Harrison was honored at the Hall in September 2003 as an NFL Most Valuable Mom. Linda and 12 other players' mothers—including Marilyn Porcher (Detroit defensive end Robert Porcher), Mary Taylor (Seattle cornerback Bobby Taylor) and Virginia Davis (Carolina running back Stephen Davis)—were inducted into the Campbell's Chunky Soup Most Valuable Mom exhibit.

Linda was one of the founding members of the Professional Football Players Mothers Association. She served as the group's secretary and national event coordinator.

The association seeks to promote their sons' personal development, positive images and charitable initiatives, present seminars for families and involve itself in community programs.

Catch Me If You Can

Marvin Harrison was on his way out, headed down an RCA Dome hallway. He was alone, but not lonely; happy, but not bubbly; getting away, but not fleeing.

"Marvin," a reporter walking in the opposite direction, toward the locker room, ventured. "Got a minute?"

Harrison's head came up. He flashed a grin.

"What's going on?" he asked.

What's going on? Why wait? What to talk about?

Two hours earlier, Harrison had made one of the more spectacular touchdown catches you're ever going to see. It was the setup play in a breakthrough 33-7 victory, one that provided a 17-3 halftime lead against a Tennessee team that had owned the Colts and the AFC South division in which both compete.

No matter. Harrison didn't linger. He seldom does. He was out the locker room door, headed for freedom, not awaiting the media horde and its postgame inquisition.

Harrison shrugged. He flashed another grin.

"I just try to make the hard catch routine," he said, and he was off again, off into the night.

Making difficult catches was routine for Marvin Harrison (88). (Matt Detrich/*The Indianapolis Star*)

Pinning down Harrison, much less stopping him, was like catching quicksilver. You weren't going to do it, and if you did, you didn't hold him long. He would squirt away again.

While Harrison largely succeeded in rendering the spectacular routine, there were exceptions, as was the case that September Sunday.

The Colts' wide receiver split wide, right, on the play and was covered by Pro Bowl cornerback Samari Rolle. Harrison made a double move. He broke downfield, then slowed as if to curl. Rolle looked back for the football. Harrison exploded past him.

It is testimony to Rolle's athleticism that he recovered enough to push Harrison, but the wide receiver maintained his balance, and in one flowing motion stretched for a ball Peyton Manning put where only he could catch it, and then tip-tapped both feet down just inside the sideline.

It was a 35-yard touchdown. It was ballet.

"It was the best catch anybody's made when I've been on him," said Rolle, a six-year veteran.

"It was ho-hum," said Harrison.

Throw Me the Ball

Ho-hum is what Marvin Harrison did again three weeks later, during a *Monday Night Football* encounter at Tampa Bay. The defending Super Bowl champions' top-ranked defense was allowing an average of 15 completions and 106 passing yards a game. Harrison had 11 catches for 176 yards and two touchdowns in the Colts' 38-35 overtime victory.

Why get excited? It was the kind of performance Harrison rehearses every day in practice with his flat-out, 10,000-rpm efforts. It's what he trains himself to do. It's what he expects.

It's why he caught 143 passes in 2002, more than any other receiver has caught in any season in NFL history. It's why he didn't celebrate touchdowns with spikes, taunts or dance steps. No flashy jewelry. No tattoos. No trash talking. No self-promotion. It's why television analyst John Madden called him "the silent dominator."

Harrison was always thinking about the next touchdown, not the last one.

"He's a perfectionist," said the person who knows the man behind the facemask best, his mom, Linda Harrison. "He was always a perfectionist. His schoolwork had to be perfect. You go into his house, you'd think you were at a lady's house. His house is immaculately kept."

Clean up the rough edges during the week. Make tidy work of an opponent's best cover man and imaginative double-teams on Sunday. Keep the football house in the same order as the residence.

It's the only way to operate.

"I try to do everything right," said Marvin. "And when I don't, I don't need anybody to tell me. That's the only way to do it: Do it correct, and every time."

Man of the House at a Tender Age

Marvin lost his father and his mom, Linda, lost her husband at a point of great vulnerability. Linda was 21 when a congenital disease took Charles Harrison. Marvin was two.

The family lived in North Philly, where life was lived to the accompaniment of the siren's wail, and gunshots and gang fights were too common. The area then was Philadelphia's most desperate.

Linda worked nine to five in an insurance company's claims department and later as an administrative assistant at a job placement firm. She worked nights and weekends as a hairdresser. She had a daughter, Ayisha, and another son, Jibril, but she never remarried. She just kept moving.

"I grieved a little bit," she said, "but I had a child to raise. You have to keep moving. It was a struggle, but you make do."

Marvin was young, but he was big brother, the man of the house. He supervised. He did laundry. He cleaned. He learned to be responsible, resourceful, orderly.

Linda is one of seven children. Her family closed ranks around her and Marvin.

While Linda was working, Marvin was with his grandparents, his uncles and aunts. Family was paramount. Its bonds were bulletproof. They became Marvin's world and remain his refuge.

Marvin provided generously for his mother. He was fiercely protective of his extended family. He was fiercely private, often aloof. As warm as Harrison can be on occasion, he was a master of the conversational stiff-arm.

"He doesn't have a lot of really close friends," testified Linda. "His family are his close friends. He doesn't bring a lot of people into his private world."

Roger that, his teammates said.

"I don't know of many people that know Marv," said wide receiver Reggie Wayne.

"A lot of guys go out, go to night clubs, go to bars or malls or movie theaters," said tight end Marcus Pollard. "I've seen him out one time, at Best Buy, looking for some movies on a Tuesday.

"He does his own thing. Lone wolf."

Afterburners Are an Afterthought

It's convention to refer to an NFL wide receiver, then make note of his 40-yard dash time. Not Marvin Harrison. If you heard a 40 time attached to him, be skeptical. He wasn't timed since he was at Syracuse University.

No need. Harrison had what Peyton Manning calls "special speed."

"You just tell me to run whatever it is," said Harrison. "I can do it. Speed has never been my problem."

Carrying on a Proud Tradition

By any measure, Peyton Manning and Marvin Harrison were among the top pitch-and-catch combinations in league history. They also were successors to a legend.

No one did it better than John Unitas and Raymond Berry, Hall of Fame members who played together for the Baltimore Colts from 1956 through 1967. Football has undergone immense changes over the past 40 years, but the dynamics of the exceptional quarterback-receiver combination have not.

Take the 1958 NFL championship game. A 17-14 Colts deficit. A little more than a minute to play. No timeouts. The league's top defense across the line of scrimmage.

Unitas called two plays in the huddle. Berry was the primary receiver on both, but when he split wide to run a 12-yard "L," a square-in, New York Giants linebacker Harland Svare lined up on him, facemask to facemask. Given the rules of the day, Berry was not going to run a 12-yard in, not while wearing Svare like a necktie.

Berry faked a quick out-cut, then slanted sharply under Svare. Unitas's pass hit Berry in stride for 25 yards, the key play in the Colts' drive to the tying field goal. Baltimore won "the greatest game ever played" in overtime.

"It wasn't until 30 years later that I realized the significance of what we did," said Berry, who caught 12 passes for

178 yards that day. "One time John and I got talking about what we would do if they walked a linebacker up on me. We arrived at the adjustment that we'd convert it to a slant, and every once in a while, when we were working together, we'd rehearse that kind of thing.

"But I don't think we'd even talked about it in the two weeks before the Giants game."

Berry and Unitas didn't even have a hand signal. Only a surpassing sense of one another and a shared instinct for the game. Harrison and Manning had it, too.

"We both see the same thing," said Harrison. "I think that's what makes Peyton and me that much better together: We both see the same thing before it happens."

Manning might have called a play in the huddle, then looked at Harrison and said, "Philadelphia '99" or "Miami 2000" or "Kansas City 2001." Nothing further was necessary.

Harrison recalled the play that resulted in a touchdown or big play in the game cited. He adjusted his route.

The same thing happened at the line of scrimmage. Manning made his reads. Harrison made his. The "Miami 2000" cue or an exchange of hand signals might have followed.

"With all the different defenses teams put in, you might call a play that's a great man-to-man play, but if they're playing zone, it's horrible," said Manning. "You've got literally no chance. You have to adjust."

One play can turn a game, even a season. The best quarterback-receiver combinations make them, because they're ready for anything.

*The noise you hear is Marvin Harrison as one of the NFL's premier wide receivers. (Steve Healey/*The Indianapolis Star*)*

Mutual Admiration Society

Raymond Berry, the country kid from Paris, Texas, and Marvin Harrison, the city kid from Philadelphia, have never met, but they would like one another. Harrison would love the professionalism and work ethic that characterized Berry's career. Berry loves the understated excellence with which Harrison played.

They're both old-fashioned, and proud of it.

"When I watch Marvin play, I see a guy who's thinking football and keeping his mind on the game and not being a showboat," said Berry, whose many Colts receiving records fell to Harrison. "Hallelujah. I'm just glad to see a guy like him in the position he's in because he's a real credit to the game."

The Class of His Class

By any standard, the 1996 NFL draft could be described as "receiver-rich." The New York Jets made Keyshawn Johnson the first pick. Terry Glenn went to the New England Patriots on the seventh. The St. Louis Rams grabbed Eddie Kennison at No. 18 and the Buffalo Bills used the 24th selection on Eric Moulds.

Marvin Harrison? Everyone liked him, but the consensus was that he was a bit small and not real strong. The Colts stole him at No. 19.

Harrison was the most productive receiver of the 1996 class. Johnson (814 receptions, 10,571 yards, 64 TDs) was second, 288 catches, 4,009 yards and 64 touchdowns behind Harrison.

Try Topping This One

Marvin Harrison made so many spectacular catches that his teammates and coaches were almost inured to them. Almost.

Some were just so good, so ludicrously over-the-top, you've-got-to-be-kidding-me sensational, that everyone's mouths fell open.

Like the one he made during the taut 29-27 victory at Tennessee in 2003 that just about assured the Colts of the AFC South title and home field during the first round of the playoffs.

The play was a deep post. Harrison not only was covered, he was double-covered. Cornerback Samari Rolle and safety Tank Williams were on Harrison like aftershave.

No matter. No one wanted the ball like Harrison wanted the ball. He exploded. He dove, stretched, laid out parallel to the turf. He got the fingers of his right hand on the football, and in one flowing motion, pulled it in and rotated his body to shield it from the impact as he hit the ground.

Forty-two yards. It set up the decisive touchdown. It ranked with the most sensational catches in NFL history. It was still running on *SportsCenter* at season's end. They'll show it for years.

Atlanta cornerback Ray Buchanan saw it on the highlights, and again while studying film for the Falcons' visit to the RCA Dome the following Sunday.

"He's sick. He's a freak," pronounced Buchanan. "We might have to check his DNA. He might be an alien."

Harrison didn't hang around to talk about it. Reporters seeking a comment had to go out to the parking lot and get him off the team bus.

Exiting a Colt

A player who was so at home and electric on the playing field but so reserved and unapproachable away from it, saw his career end February 24, 2009. The Colts terminated Harrison's contract. He became an unrestricted free agent, but never signed with another team.

"I'm indebted to him," Manning said when he learned of Harrison's release. "I'm sad he won't be here. There's no way I would be at the place I am right now if I hadn't played with Marvin for 11 years. In my opinion, he's always going to be a Colt."

Harrison holds franchise records for receptions (1,102), receiving yards (14,580) and receiving touchdowns (128). In 2011, the team added Harrison to its Ring of Honor, and in 2016, he was inducted into the Pro Football Hall of Fame.

A Return to the Spotlight

The reticent Colt found himself on the NFL's grandest stage. On February 6, 2016, Harrison gained entry into the Pro Football Hall of Fame as a member of the Class of 2016. His bronze bust found a home in Canton, Ohio, on August 6 of that year.

It was during the enshrinement ceremony that Harrison, who routinely avoided publicity during his 13-year career, finally welcomed it. The running joke leading up to the event was the length—or brevity—of Harrison's acceptance speech. The Hall of Fame "suggests" an enshrinee limit his speech to 12 to 15 minutes.

Robert Mathis, Harrison's long-time Colts teammate, couldn't imagine Harrison pushing the limit.

"No, and I'm taking bets on that," he said with a smile. "Seven minutes, tops. Five to seven minutes."

Wrong. So very wrong.

That became clear when Harrison settled behind the podium and scanned the thousands of fans—including dozens of his former teammates—in attendance.

"Before I begin, I just want to say one thing," he said. "I've broken a lot of records, I've held a lot of records, and records are made to be broken. But my current Hall of Famers that I sit here on my left and my right, I just want to tell you one thing: I'm not going to break the record to have the shortest speech in Hall of Fame history.

"That's not going to happen."

The Quiet One went on to offer more of himself than he ever had. He thanked his family for supporting him along the way and shared how much he's enjoyed being able to spend quality time with sons Marvin Jr. and Jett during his post-NFL life. He thanked Joe Ferrero, a teacher at Philadelphia's Roman Catholic High School, for constantly pushing and motivating him.

And Harrison thanked his Speech 101 teacher at Syracuse University—Mrs. Johnson—for preparing him for what would be the most demanding speech of his life.

"The first day of class she said to me, the class is going to be divided up into three parts—50 percent attendance, 25 percent exams and 25 percent presentation," Harrison said. "And I told her right away . . . 'I'm going to do the best I can do to get 75 percent in this class.' And she said, 'What do you mean?'"

Harrison informed her "I'm not going to give a speech . . . that's not what I do."

He finally relented.

"As the year went on, I did the class, I did the course and I passed the class," Harrison said. "She said to me, 'Marvin, some day you're going to look back on this day and thank me because you're going to have to give the biggest speech of your life, so you might as well do it now.'

"So I want to thank Mrs. Johnson for that."

Chapter Six

EDGERRIN JAMES

First Impressions

The city of Indianapolis didn't exactly embrace Edgerrin James. Not at first.

When he came to town in mid-February for the 1999 National Football Scouting Combine, the media spotted a running back prospect with dreadlocks. They cornered James in the lobby of the Crowne Plaza, confident they were directing questions at Ricky Williams, the Heisman Trophy winner out of Texas. Nope, it was a junior-eligible halfback out of the University of Miami.

Then came April 17. Draft day. And what Colts fans hoped was another case of mistaken identity.

Speculation leading up to the draft focused on the Colts selecting Williams. They laid the groundwork for the acquisition of another workhorse by trading Marshall Faulk to the St. Louis Rams. Everyone expected Williams and wanted Williams.

With the fourth overall pick, the Colts gave them James. Reaction around Indy was swift and mostly hostile. An unscientific sampling of callers to the local newspaper showed that people disapproved of the selection by a 10-to-1 margin.

Ron Haverstock played college football at Penn State, where he shared a room with Hall of Fame running back Franco Harris. He watched the draft unfold at Montgomery Inn, a local restaurant/bar, with approximately 1,000 other Colts fans. He wasn't pleased.

"They had an opportunity today to make a pick as big as last year, with Peyton Manning," said Haverstock. "As much as I believe in Peyton Manning, that's how little I believe in James."

Ouch.

James learned he, not Williams, was in the Colts' crosshairs when they called him just prior to making the selection. He was sharing the draft-day festivities with family and friends at Lozano's Restaurant & Sports Bar in his hometown of Immokalee, Florida. He was elated at the decision and unapologetic to those who were upset he wasn't Ricky Williams.

"Somebody had a lot of guts to pull the trigger and pick me [ahead of Williams]," James said. "I'm just going to be myself. The way I work, it's going to show what I'm capable of doing. I won't let the team down in any fashion."

Nothing to It

Edgerrin James missed the first three weeks of his rookie training camp. There was business to tend to—his seven-year, $49 million contract that included $9.85 million in

Edgerrin James introduced himself to the NFL by winning league rushing titles in each of his first two seasons. (Rob Goebel/*The Indianapolis Star*)

immediate bonuses—before the Colts' 1999 first-round draft pick could get down to the business of becoming the centerpiece of the team's rushing attack.

So much for the importance of training camp. James made up for lost time, and gave everyone a glimpse of what was to come, when he first stepped on the field. It was the Colts' third preseason game, ironically in New Orleans. On the Saints' sideline, in street clothes and nursing a sprained ankle, was Ricky Williams, the running back everyone believed the Colts would draft instead of James.

James played sparingly, but spectacularly. He was on the field for three series and carried the ball only 10 times. There were 16- and 12-yard touchdown runs, 77 yards in all. And there was emotion from a player who generally keeps himself composed on the football field. He punctuated each TD run by looking up in the stands and pointing his index fingers at the crowd.

"It was only a preseason game," said James, "so you can't get all caught up in that."

Team president Bill Polian attempted to downplay James's snazzy start.

"He's going to be terrific, but for people to think he's going to do it tomorrow, no," said Polian. "It can't happen. If it does, it's far more the exception than the rule."

Exception noted. James became the 13th rookie to lead the league in rushing (1,553 yards), the first since the Rams' Eric Dickerson in 1983. Then, in 2000, he became only the fifth player in NFL history to win the rushing title in each of his first two seasons. James's 1,709 yards were a franchise record.

Easy Does It

They told him it was just the next step, from college to the pros. A big one, to be sure, but nothing he couldn't handle. Randy Moss told Edgerrin James. So did Deion Sanders and Cornelius Bennett.

James listened. And agreed.

"I was talking to Randy Moss and he told me [the NFL] wasn't as big as they blew it up to be," James said as he prepared for his rookie season with the Colts. "I remember that. I've talked to Deion, Cornelius, a lot of guys. They tell me it's more mental than before.

"The main difference is every week you have to bring it. But it's not what it's blown up to be. There are no easy wins. You just have to go out and play hard every week. It's just a matter of staying tuned in and doing what you do best."

A Chevy Man

Edgerrin James doesn't want for wheels. Parked on his personal car lot are a Bentley and an ivory Cadillac Escalade. Each is loaded.

Force him to choose a ride, though, and he's likely to snuggle up to his 1975 Chevrolet Impala. He bought it from his brother while attending the University of Miami. It cost him $1,000. It's worth so much more. The Hurricanes orange and green Chevy has a nitro-fueled, 502-horsepower engine, big rims and a sound system that would rival most of the nightclubs he frequents.

James described the Bentley as "one of those trend-type things."

"My Chevy," he said, "it's going to go to my kids, and my kid's kids."

What a Ride!

Leave it to Edgerrin James to make a grand entrance.

It was time to report for the 2002 training camp at Rose-Hulman Institute of Technology in Terre Haute, and the Colts' veteran running back needed a lift from his home in Indianapolis. It seems his driver's license had been suspended for a month for an accumulation of traffic violations in Florida.

What to do? Call a taxi, that's what. So James did. While other players pulled up at the players' dormitory in their luxury cars and SUVs, James pulled himself out of a Yellow Cab. It was cab No. 42 and driven by Yancy Jackson. It cost James and wide receiver Reggie Wayne, his teammate and riding mate, $150.

"This is what happens when they take your license," James said, smiling broadly. "I told coach [Tony] Dungy I'd get here with no problems."

A South Florida Guy

Edgerrin James continually drew attention to himself by spending as little time as possible in Indianapolis during the offseason. With the exception of 2002, when he was coming off reconstructive knee surgery, he participated in the team's mandatory three-day mini-camp. But when it came to the voluntary offseason program and summer school, James preferred to be elsewhere. And generally was.

No offense intended to the Indianapolis Chamber of Commerce, but James is a south Florida kind of guy. Miami, Immokalee, Naples.

"With my lifestyle and everything," he said, "I'm not going to be up [in Indianapolis]. I've tried to be up there. I'd rather be down [in Miami]. I like to stay up and have fun. I'm young. I want to enjoy my life.

"Just to make everybody happy I'm not going to go to Indianapolis. Clubs close at two o'clock [in the morning] and I'm supposed to go home? Don't think so. We gonna stay out 'til tomorrow."

Giving Back

The two buildings once were hangouts for druggies and troublemakers who roamed the streets in Immokalee, Florida. Edgerrin James knows from personal experience. "I grew up fast, real fast," he said. "I done did all that. But I never made it as my story."

No, his story includes helping break the cycle of despair in his hometown. James invested his time and own money into turning the structures that formerly housed so much peril into a "Funhouse" for the neighborhood youngsters and a weight room for himself.

Drugs remain prevalent in Immokalee, but not at James's Funhouse. "They know it's off limits," he said.

The Funhouse serves as a small-scale YMCA for kids who are unable to frequent the real deal. There's a pool table, a TV room with a big-screen TV, stereo system, couches, and a game room. Out back, James installed a regulation basketball court that's in continual use.

"He's done a great job of getting a lot of kids off the street, whether they play athletics or not," said Immokalee

HS coach John Weber. "It's probably more important for the ones who aren't going to play athletics."

As for the weight room, it cost $50,000 to refurbish and allows James to work out whenever the mood strikes. "When I'm home," he said, "I have 24-hour access."

The "Stretch" Play

Edgerrin James had run past them all during his first five seasons with the Colts: Alan Ameche, Lydell Mitchell, Lenny Moore, Eric Dickerson, Marshall Faulk. He's the franchise's career rushing leader, a two-time NFL rushing champion.

And to think so much of the credit can be traced to a simple play, the base play of the Colts' ground game.

"We call it 'stretch,'" said quarterback Peyton Manning. "'Stretch right' or 'stretch left.'"

The play is designed to stretch a defense as it pursues along the line of scrimmage. As it flows toward the sideline, blockers attempt to create a seam. Ideally, they pinch their defensive player inside. If the play works as offensive coordinator Tom Moore designed it, James gets to the corner and only has one defender to beat. He also has the option of cutting the play up inside if he notices a running lane.

"You want to get outside and get [the defense] flowing," said James. "When you do, there's going to be a lane pop up somewhere, either early or late."

When he was first exposed to the stretch play, James fought his instincts. They told him to cut inside at the first opportunity. As he grew more comfortable with it, he grew more patient.

"I've got to be more disciplined in staying out there, staying out there, staying out there," he said.

Patience couldn't be a part of Manning's role on the play. He, after all, initiated it. James couldn't do anything until Manning took the snap from center Jeff Saturday, pivoted to one side or the other and sprinted back at an angle to deliver the handoff.

"When I get older," he said, "I might have to turn and pitch that thing."

Pitching the football rather than handing it off would eliminate one of the challenges presented to the defense by the stretch play. Manning is one of the NFL's best at carrying out play-fakes. Does he have the football? Did he give it to James? Is it a run? A pass?

"When you pitch it," said Manning, "they know right away it's not a pass."

The Colts took control of the AFC South with a 29-27 victory at Tennessee on December 7, 2003. James used the stretch play to methodically attack the Titans' perimeter, rushing 28 times for 97 yards.

The following week, in a 38-7 blowout of Atlanta, two of Manning's five touchdown passes came off play-action with the stretch play. The Colts ran the stretch play to the left side on their first play from scrimmage. Instead of sticking the football in James's hands, Manning pulled it back.

Falcons linebacker Keith Brookings hesitated, thinking run. Uncertainty also caused safety Ray Buchanan to hesitate. Manning delivered a 14-yard touchdown pass to Reggie Wayne.

"When you run it right," said James, "it keeps everybody on their heels."

Down and Out in K.C.

It was nothing more than a little twist, some pain working its way through Edgerrin James's left knee that had subsided shortly after the Colts' 35-28 win at Kansas City's Arrowhead Stadium on October 25, 2001.

James joked with teammates after taking a shower. He walked around with a slight limp, but there was no ice on his knee, no hint of what was to come.

Quarterback Peyton Manning paused as he reached James's locker.

"How is it?" he asked.

"I'll be all right," James replied.

Added coach Jim Mora: "I don't think it's serious."

But it was. It was season-ending.

With 4:26 remaining in the game, James had his left knee bent awkwardly when he was tackled by Chiefs linebacker Marvcus Patton. The damage: a torn anterior cruciate ligament. Reconstructive surgery was required and performed by noted Miami, Florida, orthopedic surgeon John Uribe on November 24.

That ended weeks of speculation and controversy surrounding the seriousness of the injury. The Colts talked in generalities regarding the extent of the damage, revealing at one point that James sustained "ligament involvement." They held out hope that James would return at some point during the season.

Hope was extinguished on November 21 when James was placed on the league's injured reserve list.

"Surgery has reached the point where these things, while not routine, have a very good chance of success," said team president Bill Polian. "We're all positive about that."

Doing It His Way

Edgerrin James always has followed his heart, done things his way. That was never more evident than during his long road back from reconstructive knee surgery.

Convinced it was in his best interest to remain in Miami and rehab, James did precisely that. He even took it to the extreme, choosing to skip the team's mandatory three-day mini-camp. In April 2002, critics questioned his motives. James shrugged. He knew what was best; the critics be damned.

"Once I'm in a comfort zone, I don't want to change anything," he said. "Right now this is what's best for me. Everything is working out just right, so I don't see any reason to go [to Indianapolis]."

It's Voluntary

A team's "voluntary" offseason workouts are voluntary in name only. Players are urged to participate. That's especially true during summer school, a three- or four-week stretch when teams are allowed to hold full-squad, non-contact drills.

Edgerrin James caused a stir during the 2001 offseason when he opted to remain in south Florida. When he wasn't working up a sweat at the University of Miami under the guidance of Hurricanes strength and conditioning coach Andrew Swayze, he was enjoying himself. Bowling until the wee hours of the morning. Piloting his 38-foot boat, aptly named Stressss Freee. Just hangin'.

James had a problem understanding that how he was spending his offseason was an issue, why his absence was so surprising.

"I only went to college for two and a half years," he said, "but I think I know the meaning of the word voluntary.

"This is the first time I haven't been there. What's the big deal? I just prefer to be down here. I got more publicity for not comin' than I did for some of what I did last year on the field. It's crazy."

Back to Arrowhead

Who would have blamed Edgerrin James for walking nervously into Kansas City's Arrowhead Stadium for an AFC divisional playoff matchup with the Chiefs on January 11, 2004? That, after all, is where his blossoming career came to an abrupt halt a little more than two years earlier. Remember October 25, 2001? The torn ACL?

Typically, James took it all in stride.

"I'm not superstitious," he said. "It's a football game. [The injury] is one of those things that was unfortunate, but it's part of the game.

"It's cool. It's probably a good thing. The last time you go there, things didn't work out. Now, you're going back and there's more on the line."

James certainly didn't dwell on what happened in '01. In a 38-31 victory that sent the Colts to the AFC championship game at New England, he rushed 26 times for 125 yards and two touchdowns.

What's in a Number?

No. 32? No. 5? The number James wore depended upon when he wore it.

When the Colts tackled their preseason schedule and during the regular season, James was No. 32 in your program. That's the number he was assigned as a rookie. He wanted No. 5, which is the number he wore at the Pop Warner level, at Immokalee High School and the University of Miami. The NFL, though, requires running backs to wear jerseys in the 20-49 range.

Instead of simply giving in, James compromised. During mini-camp, summer school and the early portion of training camp, he pulled on a No. 5 jersey.

"No. 5 was a hot number when I was growing up," James said. "One of my favorite running backs in college was Garrison Hearst. One of the baddest running backs to play at the University of Miami was Melvin Bratton. They both wore No. 5. It was always, 'Who's the baddest No. 5?'"

Mr. Fix-It

The Colts were driving for what would be Mike Vanderjagt's game-winning 27-yard field goal with less than five minutes remaining against the New York Jets. It was a time for conservative aggression. It was time for the Colts to lean heavily on Edgerrin James, their rookie workhorse.

The only problem: James had suffered a dislocated ring finger on his left hand. It pointed in the wrong direction and sent jolts of pain through his body.

The problem proved to be no problem at all. Calling Dr. James. He wrapped the fingers on his right hand around the disjointed, throbbing finger and jerked it back in to place.

"It was ugly," James said, "but we don't have too many running backs here, and this was a game we needed badly, plus a game I wanted to continue to play. I just put it back into place. This is a the type of game where you put pain aside."

After putting the pain aside, James did likewise to the Jets. On the nine-play, 35-yard drive that culminated with Vanderjagt's field goal and a 16-13 victory, James carried six times for 25 yards.

The come-from-behind win proved to be a defining moment for the Colts. It was the first of 11 consecutive victo-

Edgerrin James had no intention of changing his lifestyle or his looks. (Kelly Wilkinson/**The Indianapolis Star**)

ries that enabled them to finish the 1999 season with a 13-3 record and win the AFC East title.

Image Isn't Everything

The advice came early: Cut the dreadlocks, lose the gold teeth. Image, advisors told Edgerrin James, is everything. Hone an image that courts corporate America, they urged, and the cash will flow.

James just shook his dreads and flashed a smile that was golden.

"People are always telling me, 'You're losing all these opportunities,'" he said. "But what sense does it make if I'm not happy with what I'm doing? Why should I change who I am? My mom's got gold teeth. My brother's got gold teeth. Growing up in south Florida, you go down there, you see a lot of people with gold teeth.

"Someday, maybe, I'll take out the teeth and cut the hair. But it will be my choice."

OK, the Dreads Are Expendable

It didn't take a lucrative endorsement opportunity to convince Edgerrin James to shear his trademark dreadlocks. All it took was someone yanking on them during a game.

In the Colts' 2003 regular-season opener, a 9-6 win at Cleveland, a Browns defender brought James to a quick halt by grabbing the dreadlocks that hung below his helmet and bounced off his shoulder pads.

In Week 2, the Tennessee Titans weren't given a similar chance.

"When [the Browns] grabbed my hair," explained James, "that made me rethink. I gave in right there; I can't go through that all year. It was best for me to go ahead and chop it off."

That didn't require a trip to the barbershop. James did the honors himself, shortening his dreads by some six inches.

The Titans undoubtedly wished James had waited another week. Deprived of a handle, the Tennessee defense failed to get hold of James. He rushed 30 times for 120 yards and one touchdown. He was the team's heartbeat as the Colts handled Tennessee 33-7 after losing to the Titans in the 1999 playoffs, then being swept by them while finishing second to their AFC South brethren in 2002.

Older, Wiser

During his first two years with the Colts, Edgerrin James seldom rested on game day. He led the NFL in both rushing yards (3,262) and rushing attempts (756). His support staff basically stood around and watched. The rest of the team's running backs combined for 19 carries and 40 yards in 1999–2000.

"If I'm able to play, there's no way I'm going to accept coming out," said James. "When I come to play, I come to play. There's only 60-some snaps a game. The longest drive is 12-15 plays. Shoot, I can do that all day long."

James sang a different refrain during the Colts' 2003 run to the AFC title game. He carried a lighter load. Willingly.

"I got out of the fantasy league business," James said, referring to his prior drive to pile up daunting statistics. "Back then, it was about scoring points and getting 100-yard games.

"Now, the perspective is different. It's like, do what it takes."

That means coming out for a play, even a series, and letting Dominic Rhodes, Ricky Williams or James Mungro pound away at defenses.

Quarterback Peyton Manning noticed James's more prudent approach.

"What he has done is get a little bit smarter," said Manning. "You see him take himself out. He used to think he had to be in there every play."

Pay Up, Edge

Be careful when wagering with Edgerrin James. Oh, he'll pay up if he winds up on the short end, but not always by conventional means.

During the 2001 regular season, James made friendly wagers on the New York Yankees-Arizona World Series with linebacker Sam Sword and defensive back Rodregis Brooks. James sided with the Yankees and was forced to pony up when the Diamondbacks rallied to win Game 7. He did so by dragging two large buckets of pennies into the locker room and placing them in front of the winners' locker stalls.

There were 60,000 pennies in all—50,000 for Sword ($500) and 10,000 for Brooks. James retrieved the pennies from a local bank prior to going to the team's complex.

"I told y'all I'd have your money Monday morning," James cackled. "Here it is. I counted every one of 'em. I'm a man of my word."

Losing the Edge

James's long run as one of the Colts' "Triplets" came to a close when the team opted not to re-sign him after the 2005 season. He would sign with the Arizona Cardinals, but James's imprint in Colts' history was deep. He holds team rushing records for yards in a career (9,226), a season (1,709) and single game (219).

Owner Jim Irsay's appreciation of James's contributions were clear. After the Colts' victory over Chicago in Super Bowl XLI, Irsay made certain James—an Arizona Cardinal at the time—received a Super Bowl ring.

Chapter Seven

MIKE VANDERJAGT

Marches to His Own Beat

Mike Vanderjagt might have been the most talked-about and talked-to placekicker in NFL history. Why not? He was certifiably the most accurate and probably the most unique.

Colts defensive tackle Larry Triplett called Vanderjagt "an original."

Tight end Marcus Pollard called him "an iconoclast."

"He carries himself different on the field," said Pollard. "He's different in the locker room. Nobody dresses like him. He's just 'Mike.'"

That's a fact.

An iconoclast is someone who "attacks settled beliefs or institutions." Vanderjagt had assaulted the placekicking stereotype, the unwritten rule that his is the unspoken position.

This was not a bashful football player. He has an opinion on everything, and more often than not, an inclination to share it.

Ask him anything. Call him anything, anything but "cocky," despite the preponderance of evidence. He doesn't like that.

"I think 'cocky' is a negative term," said Vanderjagt. "Just because I say I'm good doesn't make me cocky. It just happens to be fact, really."

Man of the Moment

It has been that way most of Mike Vanderjagt's life.

He began playing organized sports as a seven-year-old. He scored seven goals in his first soccer game and as a goalie eventually reached the final cut for the Canadian National Soccer Team. As a senior at White Oaks High School in Oakville, Ontario, he averaged 31 points during basketball season. He went 23-2 as the Wildcats' starting quarterback. He was a smooth-skating center and the number one scorer for the hockey team.

"When he was about 12, he needed seven goals to be the hockey team's leading scorer," recalled Vanderjagt's mother, Celia. "We were away in the Caribbean on holiday, but when we called home to see how he did, he said everything went well.

"They won 7-0. He scored all seven goals."

When you have always been the one with the ball in your hand or the puck on your stick when the game's on the line, you learn to handle it, even relish it.

"There aren't a whole lot of people who have a job where 68,000 people are watching you and you alone," said Vanderjagt. "I mean it's a field goal unit, but when it comes down to making or missing, it's the kicker.

"I engulf it. I enjoy it. I smile sometimes at the situation I'm in. Whether it's the game-winning kick and the place is yelling uncontrollably, I stand there thinking, 'You know what? I'm in control of this whole situation.' That's what's cool about it."

Only one kicker in the NFL's 82 years has kicked a 50-yard field goal in the final seconds to send a game into overtime and another 50-yarder to win it. Vanderjagt did it on a frigid late November night in Denver during the 2002 season. He knifed a rock-hard football 54 yards through snow and sub-20-degree air with three seconds to play to tie it. He made a 51-yarder with 9:22 left in overtime to win it.

He went three for three that night, also converting a 41-yarder. It didn't matter that he was coming off a three-for-eight stretch, the worst of his six NFL seasons. Like he told quarterback Peyton Manning during pregame:

"Don't worry," said Vanderjagt. "I'll make them."

The Mouth That Roared

Ordinarily, Mike Vanderjagt kicked to win games and break records. In the weeks following the 2002 season, he kicked up a fuss.

Still stinging from the Colts' 41-0 AFC wild card loss to the New York Jets on January 4, Vanderjagt questioned the emotional commitment and leadership of quarterback Peyton Manning and head coach Tony Dungy.

Of Manning, who fell to 0-3 in the playoffs with the loss, Vanderjagt said, "Some guys have it, and some guys don't."

Dungy presided over a 6-10 to 10-6 turnaround in 2003, his first season with the Colts, but Vanderjagt, a Toronto-area native, questioned his coach's leadership style.

"Coach Dungy, he's just a mild-mannered guy," said Vanderjagt. "He doesn't get too excited; he doesn't get too down, and I don't think that works, either.

"I think you need a motivator. I think you need a guy that is going to get in somebody's face when they're not performing well enough. Peyton and Tony are basically the same guy. They work hard; they mark their Xs and Os and go out and execute. If it doesn't happen, there's nothing we can do about it."

Vanderjagt was coming off the worst season of his six-year NFL career, a 23-for-31 run that included a three-for-eight streak at midseason. He held out little hope for the team's immediate future.

"I'm not a real big Colts fan right now," he said. "I just don't see us getting better."

Caught in the Backlash

Mike Vanderjagt issued a statement through his agent a few days later saying he regretted his comments and that he didn't intend to insult Peyton Manning or Tony Dungy, but the firestorm had been loosed. For 10 days, talk radio and just about every other sports forum raged on the subject. Some Colts fans condemned Vanderjagt; others commended him.

Dungy had an earnest conversation with his kicker, after which he said, "If that is truly what he thinks and he doesn't want to play here because he doesn't think we can win, then he shouldn't be here."

Manning responded loudly, and there was no mistaking his feelings.

"Here we are," Manning told ABC-TV reporter Lynn Swann during a sideline interview at the Pro Bowl in Honolulu. "I'm at my third Pro Bowl, I'm about to throw a touchdown to Jerry Rice, we're honoring the Hall of Fame, and we're talking about our idiot kicker who got liquored up and ran his mouth off.

Mike Vanderjagt (left) and Peyton Manning traded verbal barbs following the 2002 season. (Matt Kryger/*The Indianapolis Star*)

"...What has the sports world come to? We are talking about idiot kickers. He has ruined kickers for life.

"The sad thing is, he's a good kicker. He's a good kicker. But he's an idiot."

The furor finally began to subside after Vanderjagt and Manning exchanged apologies.

The players "talked as friends, both of us with our tails between our legs, I guess," said Vanderjagt, who was vehement in his denial that alcohol had anything to do with his inflammatory comments and admitted that club president Bill Polian, "ripped me a new one...and rightfully so."

Said Manning, "We both know we screwed up."

The players declared the incident over, and both came back to have their finest seasons in 2003. Manning shared the NFL's Most Valuable Player Award with Tennessee quarterback Steve McNair. Vanderjagt converted all 37 of his field goal attempts to run his streak to a league-record 41. He was elected to the Pro Bowl for the first time and the Colts went 14-5 and reached the AFC championship game.

Both had the last word. Both got it right.

"Game Day" Made Persistence Pay

The controversy with Peyton Manning and Tony Dungy was unique, but it wasn't Mike Vanderjagt's first go-around with hard times. As a senior at West Virginia University, he missed five field goals and five point-after kicks. NFL teams stayed away in droves. He didn't get a single expression of interest, not a lone phone call.

He was drafted by the Canadian Football League's Saskatchewan franchise. He won the punting job but missed a practice to be in his sister's wedding. The Roughriders cut him. He was signed by Toronto, then released. He was in and out of camps. He went to the Arena Football League's Minnesota Fighting Pike, where one of his kickoffs sailed wide, into the stands. That's an AFL no-no. He was cut again.

Vanderjagt sold shoes for a time at Koenig's Sport Goods in Huntington, West Virginia. He made five dollars an hour until Toronto called again. He signed for $41,000 Canadian, about $27,000 this side of the border.

The 1996 Grey Cup, the Super Bowl of Canadian football, was played in Hamilton, 15 minutes from Vanderjagt's home. It was played in a blizzard. He made nothing during the pregame. He missed nothing during the game. The Argonauts won and Vanderjagt's five-for-five performance earned him Canadian MVP honors.

It surprised no one.

Vanderjagt always was one to struggle and wander when it didn't matter, when the heat wasn't on. That's why teammates called him "Game Day" in Toronto. He was 14 for 14 in the playoffs.

"He was terrible in practice," Paul Masotti, then a wide receiver and Vanderjagt's roommate and sometimes holder, now the Argonauts' director of player personnel. "He always missed them in practice but hit them in games.

"There's no hiding the fact that he likes the limelight. He knows if he puts one through from 54 yards, he's going to be there."

A Breed Apart

Tony Dungy spent a quarter of a century in the NFL as a player and coach, and he can think of only a few players whose confidence and carriage approached Mike Vanderjagt's.

They include Pittsburgh defensive end Dwight White, who crowed that Dallas defensive linemen Harvey Martin and Randy White wouldn't get near Steelers quarterback Terry Bradshaw in Super Bowl XIII. White huffed and puffed and did so with bravado.

"They were Neiman Marcus and we were Penney's," recalled Dungy, a rookie safety, "but we were going to Neiman Marcus with our Super Bowl money."

Sure enough, Pittsburgh won, 35-31, and Bradshaw passed for a Super Bowl record four touchdowns. The Steelers' winner's shares were $18,000. Dallas settled for $9,000 a player.

One other player comes to mind when Dungy considers Vanderjagt, the inimitable John "Frenchy" Fuqua, a Steelers running back who favored rakish fur coats and platform shoes whose glass heels contained water and live goldfish.

"Mike would have fit in with those guys real well," said Dungy.

Silence Is Golden

Ever wonder what it's like to be out there, on the field, after the inevitable timeout, waiting while the field goal team sets up, the signals are called and the football comes spiraling back from long-snapper Justin Snow to holder Hunter Smith?

What of the sound and fury, the taunts from the opponent, the screams from the stands, the wind in your earhole?

Mike Vanderjagt heard none of it. No noise. No nerves. No crowd. No opponent. No fluttery stomach or parched mouth or moist palms. No outcome or consequences. No yesterday or tomorrow.

He was wrapped in a tight cocoon of concentration.

"I don't hear anything," he said. "Something shuts everything out. Your whole concentration is on the ball and Justin's hands, waiting for him to snap it to Hunter. And it's 1.3 seconds as quiet as us sitting here right now."

An Adrenaline Junkie

What set Mike Vanderjagt apart from most of us, and from most professional athletes even, is that his orientation wasn't one of fearing failure, it was seeking success. A crucial kick isn't a threat, it's an opportunity.

"Unlike most people, he's able to transform his nervousness into excitement and that into performance," said Hunter Smith, the Colts' punter and holder and one of Vanderjagt's best friends.

Vanderjagt enjoys the moment, wraps himself within it.

"That's the objective," said Chris Carr, a sports psychologist and team performance coordinator for Major League Baseball's Kansas City Royals who works with several Colts.

"An athlete performs best when he or she is able to get into 'flow state,' where absorption with the task at hand is complete.

*One of the most accurate kickers in NFL history puts his own spin on his successful kicks. (Rob Goebel/*The Indianapolis Star*)*

"People who are in flow state on a regular basis have the ability to translate a potential threat into an enjoyable challenge."

It's one of the most tired cliches in sport, but it is irrefutably rooted in sound theory: "I'm just going to go out and have fun."

That's quarterback Brett Favre, throwing, running, laughing, grinning, winning. That's Vanderjagt, converting 41 field goal attempts in succession.

When Houston players taunted him while he waited through a timeout during the Colts' 2003 regular-season finale, Vanderjagt responded as he always does. He enjoyed the moment. He grinned. He rubbed his thumb and fingers together.

"Money," he told the Texans, "I'm money."

Vanderjagt's 43-yard kick split the uprights at the gun to give the Colts a 20-17 victory and the AFC South championship.

Wide Right...and Long Gone

The end came abruptly, and disastrously, for the most accurate placekicker in Colts history. Vanderjagt's final attempt for the team came with 17 seconds remaining in a 21-18 loss to the Pittsburgh Steelers in a 2005 AFC Divisional playoff game. His 46-yard field goal sailed wide right, ending the Colts postseason and ending Vanderjagt's decorated career with the team.

He was released a few weeks later.

Vanderjagt remains the most successful kicker in team history. He holds club records with points (995) and field-goal accuracy (87.5), and set an NFL record by converting 42 consecutive field-goal attempts from 2002–04.

Through the 2016 season, Vanderjagt's 86.466 percentage ranked fifth in NFL history.

Chapter Eight

MOMENTS TO REMEMBER

Harbaugh's Unanswered Prayer

Jim Harbaugh thought his prayer, one delivered for a city and a franchise, had been answered. It looked as if Aaron Bailey, somewhere in the collection of Colts and Steelers and general mayhem that was the Pittsburgh end zone, had snatched Harbaugh's "Hail Mary" pass on the final play of the AFC championship game after the 1995 regular season.

"I thought he caught it," Harbaugh said.

That's what Brian Stablein's body language indicated. Looking down at Bailey, who was horizontal in the Pittsburgh end zone, Stablein's raised hands—touchdown!!—sent a shiver through Harbaugh's body, not to mention the sellout crowd at Three Rivers Stadium.

Harbaugh was 40 yards from the action. Too far away to know for sure. He turned his eyes to the scoreboard, which was flashing a replay.

The Colts try in vain to convince the officials that Aaron Bailey (80) caught Jim Harbaugh's Hail Mary pass in the 1995 AFC championship game. (Guy Reynolds/*The Indianapolis Star*)

"I saw the replay," he said, "and I still thought he caught it."

A second replay was shown. Then another.

"About the third time I saw the replay," said Harbaugh, "it looked like it hit the ground."

It did.

Instead of a 29-yard touchdown, a dramatic victory over the Steelers, a berth in Super Bowl XXX and a place in NFL lore as the franchise that produced one of the most scintillating plays in postseason history, the Colts were left with a 20-16 loss.

So close. So painfully close.

"Somehow it got loose," said Bailey, who saw the football rest on his midsection for a nanosecond before slipping to the turf.

"You can't come any closer than that right there to the Super Bowl," said Harbaugh, who passed for 267 yards and one touchdown.

An hour after the near miss, defensive tackle Tony

McCoy still had a difficult time accepting a play that ended one of the most endearing postseason runs in franchise history.

"On that last play," he said, "I thought we had it. The crowd got quiet, and I think they thought we had it for a second, too."

Immaculate Reception II

It was nearly as immaculate a reception as the original. And how appropriate that the Pittsburgh Steelers would be on hand for the encore.

A 54-yard touchdown pass from quarterback Mike Pagel to wide receiver Ray Butler, with a little help from Steelers cornerback Sam Washington, rallied the Colts to a 17-16 win over Pittsburgh in the eighth game of the 1984 season.

The unlikely chain of events had coach Frank Kush and so many others scratching their collective heads. *What was that?!?*

"It was a miraculous play," said Kush.

An Immaculate Reception? Oops. That one was taken. Remember Steelers running back Franco Harris scooping up a ricocheted pass from quarterback Terry Bradshaw and rambling 60 yards for a touchdown in a first-round win over Oakland in the 1972 playoffs?

Kush dubbed Butler's carbon-copy catch the "Serendipity Play."

"The football god was on our side," he said.

Pagel rolled to his right to elude pressure and delivered a pass intended for wide receiver Bernard Henry. Washington was in perfect position and tipped the football—once, twice—but couldn't control it. Butler could. He ran under the second deflection and completed the 54-yard touchdown with 34 seconds remaining.

"The catch was easy," Butler said. "It seemed the ball was just sort of hanging there in the air for me. As soon as I caught it, I knew we had six points. There was nobody around who could catch me."

Marino to Emtman?

Miami quarterback Dan Marino threw 420 touchdown passes. That doesn't include the one he pitched to Steve Emtman.

The first overall pick in the 1992 draft, Emtman was a defensive end for the Colts whose specialty was tackles and quarterback sacks. But in the seventh game of his rookie season, he went on the offensive and upstaged Marino and the Dolphins at Joe Robbie Stadium.

The Colts led 24-20 with less than a minute remaining, but Marino drove the Dolphins to a fourth and goal at the Colts' seven-yard line. Emtman denied Miami when Marino's last pass attempt of the afternoon stuck in his hands for an interception near the line of scrimmage. Rather than simply fall to the ground and end the game, Emtman got his 6'4", 290-pound body moving forward. He outran everyone who bothered to give chase for a 90-yard touchdown, then retired to the Colts' bench, where he strapped on an oxygen mask.

"What a marvelous play," said coach Ted Marchibroda.

Marvelous Harrison

There had been so many catches that defied logic, so many that required a rub of the eyes and a second look. Even a third.

Yet each of Marvin Harrison's career receptions lined up behind the one he grabbed against the Tennessee Titans in Nashville during the 2003 season. It covered 42 yards, produced a first down—Harrison waved his teammates to join him downfield after he popped up off the ground—and set up the decisive touchdown in the Colts' 29-27 win.

Dom Anile, the Colts' director of football operations, was impressed. He sought out Harrison after the game.

"Marvin," he said, "I've been in this game for a lot of years. And I'm telling you, that's the greatest catch I've ever seen."

Harrison ran a deep post. Tennessee Pro Bowl cornerback Samari Rolle and safety Tank Williams offered tight coverage. Quarterback Peyton Manning was undeterred by the double team and still considered Harrison his best option. But Manning's pass seemed too long, certainly out of reach.

"When I saw it up in the air," said Harrison, "I thought it was too far. I'm just thinking, 'Run as hard as you can.' I can't really describe it."

Initially, neither could coach Tony Dungy. He, too, thought the ball had been overthrown and was talking with wide receiver Brandon Stokley.

"Brock Huard had to tell me he caught it," Dungy said with a smile.

Harrison went horizontal, stretching his body and extending his right arm like Plastic Man. He snatched the football with his right hand and rolled onto his right side to cushion his contact to the ground and protect the ball.

"It was phenomenal," Dungy said after finally seeing the replay.

It was the best of an incredible collection.

Extraordinary Homecoming

Be honest. You turned off the TV when Ronde Barber gave Tampa Bay a 35-14 lead with 5:09 remaining in the fourth quarter by returning a Peyton Manning interception 29 yards for a touchdown.

It was October 6, 2003, ABC's *Monday Night Football* and Tony Dungy's homecoming/birthday. But some things are too painful to watch.

"If it was 11 o'clock on the East Coast and it was 35-14," Dungy admitted, "I think I probably would have [turned it off]. I would have been shocked in the morning then."

Shocked that he had missed one of the most dramatic comebacks in NFL history. But Dungy had a sideline view as Manning, wide receiver Marvin Harrison and the rest of the Colts became the first team ever to overcome a 21-point deficit in the final five minutes of a game and win.

"What a game," Manning said of the Colts' unlikely 38-35 overtime victory over the defending Super Bowl champion Buccaneers.

The comeback in regulation included Brad Pyatt's 90-yard kickoff return that set up a three-yard touchdown run by James Mungro, Idrees Bashir recovering the ensuing on-side kick that led to Manning's 28-yard touchdown pass to Harrison and a 52-yard Manning-to-Harrison completion that resulted in Ricky Williams's game-tying one-yard TD run with 26 seconds to play.

"Awesome," said Manning.

Then came overtime. Placekicker Mike Vanderjagt missed a 40-yard field goal, but received a mulligan when Tampa Bay defensive end Simeon Rice was penalized for an obscure "leaping" violation. On the do-over, Vanderjagt did in the Bucs. His 29-yarder appeared to be tipped at the line

*Safety Idrees Bashir (28) comes down with a fourth-quarter onside kick that helped spark the Colts' dramatic come-from-behind victory at Tampa Bay in 2003. (Matt Detrich/*The Indianapolis Star*)*

of scrimmage and definitely clipped the right upright, but tumbled over the crossbar.

"I called 'tip-bank,'" Vanderjagt smiled.

John Madden, ABC's expert commentator, called the game beyond belief.

"I've never seen or taken part in a comeback like that in my life," he said.

In the second half and overtime, the Colts scored all 38 of their points and accumulated 369 of their 455 total yards. In their three previous games, the Bucs' No. 1-ranked defense had yielded only 22 points.

"The thing about it is it was against the league's best defense," said Madden. "That's the amazing thing."

Prime-Time Player

Happy anniversary, Eric.

One year to the day after arriving in Indianapolis via a blockbuster trade—October 31, 1988—Eric Dickerson helped the Colts celebrate with one of the most dominant performances in the history of ABC's *Monday Night Football.*

The Colts annihilated Denver 55-23, and only coach Ron Meyer's compassion kept the Broncos from being completely humiliated as a sold-out Hoosier Dome and a national-television audience looked on in disbelief.

At halftime, the Colts led 45-10. Dickerson already had rushed for a club-record four touchdowns and 159 yards. Meyer approached Dickerson after the fourth TD, a 41-yard jaunt through the heart of Denver's defense in the second quarter, and asked if Dickerson wanted more. Dickerson declined to run any more or help the Colts run it up any more.

"I don't like to run up the score on people just to get yards," he said. "I felt like I had a chance for 200 yards, but it can come some other day."

Along with serving as further evidence to support Dickerson's claim of being the best running back in the NFL, the prime-time blowout helped boost the Colts' national image. It was their first home *Monday Night Football* appearance since their relocation in 1984, and they responded by piling up the most points in the history of *MNF*.

"It was a long time coming," said wide receiver Matt Bouza. "It was a game where everything—*everything*—went our way."

Snow Job

Tony Dungy's instincts told him to turn to punter Hunter Smith, play for field position, pin the Denver Broncos deep, rely on his defense.

Justin Snow told him to go for it.

Fourth and five at the Broncos' 33-yard line. Five minutes, 31 seconds into overtime. Snow falling, swirling. Temperature dropping. National television audience on Sunday night, November 24, 2002.

"My defensive instinct was to punt and back 'em up," confessed Dungy.

But before he could send Smith onto the field, Snow, the team's long snapper, convinced Dungy to call a timeout to consider another option: placekicker Mike Vanderjagt. Virtually every member of the Colts' field-goal unit found Dungy's ear.

"[They] said, 'Hey, let's go win it right here,'" Dungy said. "It was definitely against my better judgment. But I was overcome by their conviction."

Vanderjagt was the most accurate kicker in NFL history, but entered the Denver game mired in the worst slump of his career. He had missed five of his previous eight attempts.

He rediscovered his groove in snow-swept Invesco Field at Mile High. Vanderjagt nailed a 41-yard field goal in the first quarter, then equaled a career best and forced overtime by powering a 54-yarder through the uprights with three seconds remaining.

The exclamation point came on the first possession of overtime. Quarterback Peyton Manning directed the Colts to the Denver 33, where the drive stalled.

After serious sideline lobbying, Vanderjagt trotted onto the field. The conditions were of no concern. While playing for Toronto in the Canadian Football League, Vanderjagt was nine for nine on field goal attempts in two Grey Cup appearances.

"I'm talking brutal conditions," he said of his CFL days.

Vanderjagt ignored the cold, the snow, the pressure of the moment. His 51-yard field goal was true. Colts 23, Broncos 20.

Dungy had no trouble believing what he saw. Vanderjagt, he noted, "is a little extra special when the game is on the line."

But Dungy conceded he was somewhat surprised he allowed his own instincts to be trumped.

"Those guys used the whole timeout to talk me out of [punting]," he said. "I remember thinking, 'What am I doing listening to these guys when I'm supposed to be the head coach?'"

End of the Line

This wasn't the way the best season in Indianapolis Colts history was supposed to end.

Not with quarterback Peyton Manning, so infallible in orchestrating playoff victories over Denver and Kansas City, littering New England's Gillette Stadium with four interceptions.

Not with the Colts' No. 1-ranked passing attack being bullied by a Patriots defense that pushed the bounds of physicality.

Not with a 24-14 loss to New England in the 2003 AFC championship game.

But it did. One victory shy of Super Bowl XXXVIII.

"What a season and what a ride it was," owner Jim Irsay said, reassessing his team's 14-5 performance.

The ride simply ended too soon.

"No matter when the season ends, it just seems like it ends a little bit too early," noted Dungy.

The Colts entered Gillette Stadium on an incredible high. They opened the postseason with a 41-10 lacing of Denver in the RCA Dome, their first home playoff win since 1970. They were led by Perfect Peyton. The NFL's co-MVP looked the part, compiling a perfect quarterback rating (158.3) by completing 22 of 26 passes for 377 yards and five touchdowns.

"You look for your best players to play their best in big games," said Irsay.

It was more of the same when Manning led the Colts into Kansas City's Arrowhead Stadium. Manning passed for 304 yards and three more TDs. Edgerrin James rushed for 125 yards and two touchdowns. The Chiefs couldn't keep up, falling 38-31.

Next stop, Foxboro, Massachusetts.

"I think it's the two best teams in the AFC," projected Dungy.

The best was New England.

Patriots cornerback Ty Law intercepted three of Manning's passes, equaling Marvin Harrison's reception total. Safety Rodney Harrison contributed a fourth, snuffing out a Colts threat on their first possession with an end-zone interception.

Too many mistakes. Too many missed opportunities. Even so, the Colts still had a pulse with two minutes remaining. Trailing 21-14, they took possession at their own 20. There would be no miracle finish. The season ended with four incomplete passes.

The Colts walked away convinced the officiating crew allowed New England's defensive backs too much leeway. Too much grabbing, jostling, impeding. Those were observations, not excuses.

"They played like they had been in some championship games and we played like it was our first one," said Dungy. "They beat us and deserved to beat us and deserve to be in the Super Bowl."

Record Runner

Norm Bulaich wondered what took, well, *somebody* so long to expunge his name from the Colts' record book.

"I never thought I would hold the record as long as I did," he said.

Bulaich believed Eric Dickerson would obliterate his single-game club rushing record of 198 yards that was established on September 19, 1971, against the New York Jets. Maybe Marshall Faulk.

When the Colts selected Edgerrin James in the first round of the 1999 draft, Bulaich was certain it was only a matter of time before his mark changed hands. He watched as James became the first rookie since Dickerson in 1983 to win the NFL rushing title. He marveled at James's strength and speed, his stamina.

On more than one occasion, Bulaich told colleagues, "This man is going to break my record."

James obliged on October 15, 2000. He wore down Seattle's defense, rushing for 219 yards in a 37-24 victory. The record fell on the last of James's career-high 38 carries, a 25-yard gain.

"It's a great start, but I don't think it's going to be the last time I have a game like this," said James, who would go on to rush for a franchise-record 1,709 yards and defend his league rushing title. Bulaich, meanwhile, wondered if people realized the magnitude of piling up so much yardage during one afternoon. He mentioned an article in *USA Today* that chronicled James's performance.

"The article said, 'Edgerrin James easily broke Norm Bulaich's record of 198 yards,'" Bulaich said. "I went, 'Easily?' You don't realize how hard it is to get to that 200-yard mark and what it takes to get there."

Passing Fancy

Six. Could have been more.

In his second regular-season appearance in his hometown, Peyton Manning made it seem ridiculously easy in the Big Easy. Offensive coordinator Tom Moore insisted he required a second look before assessing his quarterback's performance. You know, the six touchdown passes which set a club record and fell one shy of equaling the NFL record.

"I still have to wait to see the tape," said Moore.

OK. But wasn't that a cut above?

"Everything worked," Moore allowed. "I can't explain it."

Manning pointed to the law of inevitability as it pertained to an offense teeming with such high-level talent.

"Every now and then," he said, "you're going to have a night that belongs to one team."

September 28, 2003, belonged to Manning and the Colts. The Saints were embarrassed bystanders in a 55-21 loss.

The Colts led 24-10 at halftime. Manning already had delivered three of his touchdown passes—a 17-yarder to running back Ricky Williams and 14- and 79-yarders to wide receiver Marvin Harrison.

The third quarter was little more than 15 minutes of pitch-and-catch. Manning spread three more TDs to running back Dominic Rhodes, rookie tight end Dallas Clark and another to Harrison.

There likely would have been more, but Manning didn't play in the fourth quarter. Before departing, he compiled the third perfect QB rating (158.3) of his career. St. Louis's Kurt Warner had posted two perfect games. No other active quarterback had more than one.

Chapter Nine

PLAYERS FROM THE PAST

Eric Dickerson a Mixed Bag

Greatness arrived in Indianapolis wearing wraparound goggles and wrapped in a mystifying package. Eric Dickerson was the premier running back in the NFL in the mid- and late 1980s, but also was considered self-centered and moody. He was quick with a smile or a smirk. He was graceful on the playing field, but occasionally obstinate away from the arena.

You never quite knew what you were getting.

So it was only appropriate the Colts acquired Dickerson in a blockbuster trade involving the Los Angeles Rams and Buffalo Bills on October 31, 1987. That was Halloween.

Dickerson provided instant national credibility to a relocated franchise that had yet to define itself in its new setting. He rushed for 5,194 yards in five seasons, leading the NFL in 1988 with 1,659 yards.

The Colts were 3-13 the season prior to Dickerson's arrival. They posted 9-6, 9-7 and 8-8 records in his first three seasons and earned a playoff berth in the strike-shortened '87 campaign.

"We were becoming a pretty solid, tough football team," said coach Ron Meyer, "but he elevated you to that next category where you needed a superstar to separate you from the masses. Dickerson did that. We had no other guy who could even come close."

But Dickerson's brief stint in Indianapolis was equal parts triumph and turmoil.

During the 1990 offseason, he took verbal shots at the Colts' offensive linemen, comparing running behind them to playing Russian roulette. He also fired a major salvo at Jim Irsay, referring to the team's general manager as "Daffy Duck." Dickerson twice drew four-week suspensions from the team, then on April 26, 1992, was traded to the Los Angeles Raiders for fourth- and eighth-round draft picks.

"He wanted to be a Hollywood boy," owner Robert Irsay said of sending Dickerson back to the West Coast, "so we sent him back to Hollywood."

...and a Hall of Famer

Eric Dickerson was the first Indianapolis Colts player to be enshrined in the Pro Football Hall of Fame, and when the final chapter was written, August 7, 1999, in Canton, Ohio, Dickerson was overwhelmed. His emotions bubbled to the surface during a parade prior to the induction ceremonies.

"I'm not emotional," Dickerson insisted. "I got emotional. It made every hit, every cold day I played, every practice and ache and pain all worthwhile."

Eric Dickerson was a mixed bag with the Colts and a Hall of Famer at the conclusion of his career. (The Indianapolis Star)

His path to Canton took him from Los Angeles (Rams) to Indianapolis (Colts), back to Los Angeles (Raiders), then to Atlanta (Falcons). He was dazzling to watch, difficult to deal with.

In the end, there were no regrets.

"A lot of things happened and I take responsibility for them," Dickerson said. "I was proud to wear the horseshoe on my helmet."

Bittersweet Homecoming for Jeff George

Jeff George came home on April 22, 1990, but where were the open arms and hugs? Where was the Welcome Wagon?

Shortly after general manager Jim Irsay authored a predraft trade with the Atlanta Falcons that enabled the Colts to select the former quarterback phenom at Warren Central High School with the first overall pick, a local television station asked its viewers for a reaction. It was as unflattering to George as it was unscientific. Nearly 88 percent of the respondents offered a "thumbs down" on George's return to Indianapolis.

George was undeterred.

"This is surely a lifelong dream for me," he said. "It seems like only yesterday I was coming out of high school, dreaming of playing for a team like the Indianapolis Colts. I'm a hometown guy. This is an ideal place for me."

It would take more than negative feedback from the community to temper Irsay's enthusiasm for George.

"The bottom line is we really feel this move, in the long run, is going to be a very significant one for us in the '90s," he said.

Irsay's pursuit of George intensified after he witnessed the raw, rare power in George's right arm while monitoring three workouts. Two unfolded where George's reputation first took root, then flourished—on the campus of the University of Illinois in Champaign.

During one workout, jaws dropped when George broke the monotony of throwing ins and outs and corner routes by effortlessly delivering the football 81 yards downfield.

"He'll never have to throw the ball that far, but it's nice to know he can," said Colts offensive coordinator Larry Kennan.

Disappointment and frustration were Jeff George's frequent companions with the Colts. (Kelly Wilkinson/*The Indianapolis Star*)

Cost of "Franchise QB" Mushrooms

What a difference eight years make.

The Colts signed Jeff George, the first overall pick in the 1990 draft, to a six-year, $15 million contract. It included a $3.5 million signing bonus. It was the most lucrative rookie deal in league history.

In 1998, the Colts selected University of Tennessee quarterback Peyton Manning first overall in the draft. They signed him to a six-year contract worth more than $47 million. It included an initial signing bonus of $11.6 million and an $8.6 million bonus after Manning's third season that enabled the Colts to "buy back" the final three years of the deal.

Inflation lives. In March 2004, the Colts re-signed Manning to a seven-year contract that dwarfed the combined deals it gave Manning in '98 and George in '90: $98 million with an NFL-record $34.5 million signing bonus.

Eugene Daniel Made a Difference

Eugene Daniel was a quiet Colt with modest goals. He was part of the team's first draft after its relocation from Baltimore to Indianapolis in 1984. All the Baton Rouge, Louisiana, native wanted to do was make the active roster as a rookie.

"When I first got here," Daniel said, "I never thought about playing four years, five years. I was just worried about making the team. I didn't know what to expect."

First, he made the roster. Then, he made a difference as a starting cornerback. For a very long time.

"I was blessed," Daniel said.

When Daniel's career with the Colts ended after the 1996 season, it was difficult to remember he joined the team as a ninth-round draft pick, the 205th overall selection. His 34 career interceptions trail only Bobby Boyd (57) and Don Shinnick (37) and tie Jerry Logan for third most in team history. He returned a 1995 interception against the New York Jets for a 97-yard touchdown, the longest ever by a Colt.

"When I think of Indianapolis, I can't help but think of good memories," Daniel said.

The feeling undoubtedly is mutual.

Jim Harbaugh, aka "Captain Comeback"

It was sometime during the 1995 season. Maybe in Giants Stadium or Joe Robbie Stadium, certainly when virtually everyone else had given up on the Colts.

Somewhere along the way, Jim Harbaugh, veteran quarterback, gave way to "Captain Comeback," resourceful and resilient quarterback. It was a nickname respectfully applied and methodically earned, one dramatic rally at a time.

"You just know he's gonna do something good," cornerback Ray Buchanan said of Harbaugh. "I know you shouldn't expect some of the stuff he's done, but you do."

"When he's in there," added center Kirk Lowdermilk, "you never know what's going to happen."

Much of the time, it was something good. Occasionally, it was something downright historic.

The Colts had overcome a 21-point deficit and won only once in more than four decades. They did it twice in '95, each time with Harbaugh under center.

*Quarterback Jim Harbaugh established himself as Captain Comeback and a fan favorite. (Paul Sancya/*The Indianapolis Star*)*

There was the afternoon in Giants Stadium. The New York Jets had the Colts in a 24-3 stranglehold midway through the third quarter. Looking for a spark, coach Ted Marchibroda yanked starting quarterback Craig Erickson and looked to Harbaugh.

Harbaugh's 14-yard touchdown pass to Marshall Faulk with 2:38 to play in regulation tied the game at 24-all. He then engineered a seven-play, 28-yard drive in overtime that set up Mike Cofer's game-winning 52-yard field goal.

There was the afternoon in Miami's Joe Robbie Stadium when Harbaugh rallied the Colts from a 24-3 halftime deficit to a 27-24 victory. In an eerily efficient second half, he completed 20 of 24 passes for 319 yards and two touchdowns to Floyd Turner and another to Aaron Bailey.

It was that type of cool amid chaos that enabled Harbaugh to emerge as the Colts' heart and soul in a 1995 season few will soon forget. It was a season of individual redemption and collective triumph.

Harbaugh was benched at the start of the season in favor of Erickson, an offseason acquisition engineered by owner Robert Irsay. Called on when Erickson faltered, "Captain Comeback" earned his first Pro Bowl appearance and won the NFL passing title with a career-best 100.7 quarterback rating.

The Colts followed Harbaugh's dynamic lead. They clinched their first playoff appearance since 1987 and reached the AFC championship game, where the wild ride ended with a 20-16 loss at Pittsburgh.

Marshall Faulk Was Good from the Start

He was better than most from the first time he stepped on the field. In his NFL debut, Marshall Faulk rushed for 143 yards and three touchdowns. It was September 4, 1994. The Colts were along for the ride. The Houston Oilers were run over 45-21.

"It's hard to say how good he'll be," said Oilers cornerback Cris Dishman. "But he's going to be one helluva back."

Of course he was. Faulk was a hardened survivor of New Orleans's Desire housing project. A normal day included drugs, the cracking of gunfire and, too often, kids dying too young.

Faulk was guided through the inner-city minefield by his mother, Cecile, who worked however many jobs it took to make certain her six sons had food on the table, clothes on their back, a reason to be *from* Desire and not another victim *of* it.

"My determination basically comes from my mom," said Faulk. "My mom, she never—ever—quit at anything. I have five older brothers and myself. She raised us all.

"My mom is my role model. That's who I picture myself emulating."

Faulk did his mother proud. An All-American career at San Diego State. Selected fourth overall by the Colts in the 1994 draft. Offensive Rookie of the Year. Selected to the first of three Pro Bowls as a Colt following the '94 season, and the game's MVP to boot.

The Colts were a team without direction, without a star when Faulk arrived. He gave them a healthy dose of each. He didn't look the part—5'10" and a somewhat pudgy 200 pounds. But stick the football in his hands, and sit back and enjoy the artistry.

"He's a darting, water-bug type," said Tampa Bay defensive coordinator Floyd Peters. "He's Bambi the deer bouncing around out there."

Bambi came at a steep price: a seven-year, $17.18 million contract that included a $5.1 million signing bonus. But the Colts had no doubt Faulk was worth every dollar.

"We lacked a big-play guy on offense, a guy who can become a pressure-point player who forces the defense to focus on him and stop him before they do anything else," said coach Ted Marchibroda. "Marshall is that kind of guy."

Faulk: Pay Me, or Else

Marshall Faulk was one of the premier running backs in the NFL heading into the 1999 season and demanded to be paid accordingly. Or else.

The Colts refused and insisted Faulk honor his contract. Their marquee running back didn't blink and made it clear he would boycott training camp without a new deal.

That quickly became the problem of the St. Louis Rams, who acquired Faulk for second- and fifth-round picks in the days leading up to the '99 draft.

"We knew Marshall was not coming to camp," said owner Jim Irsay, "but a bigger factor was the money issue."

"I felt like I had paid my dues there and deserved a new contract," countered Faulk. "And they felt like I didn't."

Big Plays from Ray Buchanan

All that was keeping Ray Buchanan from giving way to "Big Play Ray" was opportunity. And opportunity finally came knocking 10 games into the 1994 season.

When the Colts ventured into Miami's Joe Robbie Stadium, Buchanan made his 15th consecutive start at free safety. That changed in the third quarter when left cornerback Damon Watts yielded a 16- and 19-yard completions to Dolphins wide receiver O.J. McDuffie.

Out went Watts. Buchanan moved from safety to corner. Shortly thereafter, "Big Play Ray" stepped to the forefront.

Quarterback Dan Marino passed for 261 yards and one touchdown in Miami's 22-21 victory, but wished he could have had one of his 41 attempts back. That one was delivered in the direction of wide receiver Mark Ingram. It never reached him. Instead, Buchanan reacted as if he had been in Miami's huddle when the play was called.

"[Ingram] was lined up on the numbers, so I knew he was either going on an out-and-up or an in-and-up," he explained. "I sat on it pretty good..."

Buchanan broke on the pattern, intercepted Marino's pass and returned it 28 yards for a touchdown. In the blink of an eye, the Colts' worries at corner had been solved.

"Ray has the potential to be one of the best in the NFL," said defensive backs coach Pat Thomas. "He has the speed, the quickness, the instincts, and he's aggressive on the tackle.

"And he can make plays."

"Big Play Ray" would finish the season with eight interceptions and return three for touchdowns. Before being allowed to sign with Atlanta during the '97 offseason, Buchanan collected 16 interceptions. No other Colts defensive back had more than nine during that 64-game stretch.

Steve Emtman's Career Clouded by "What If?"

Where to start with a career that began with so much promise but ended in so much pain?

There was a torn anterior cruciate ligament in his left knee midway through 1992, his rookie season. The trifecta with his right knee in '93—torn anterior and medial collateral ligaments along with a ruptured patella tendon. A herniated disc in his neck in '94.

"Yeah," said Steve Emtman, "it was one thing after another."

When the Colts scouted Emtman prior to the '92 draft, they saw the complete package. He was a 290-pound defensive lineman who meshed speed, strength and up-field aggression. They made him the first overall pick, then envisioned what was to come.

Instead of being the cornerstone of what had been a rickety defense, Emtman was betrayed by his body. Time and again. He missed 30 of a possible 48 regular-season games during his first three years as a pro.

Emtman's career with the Colts ended prior to the '95 season, and he was out of the NFL after 1997. There were brief stints with Miami, San Francisco and Washington. And there were more injuries, most notably a compound fracture of a finger that required surgery.

If there were any regrets regarding a career that fell well short of expectations, Emtman insisted on keeping them to himself.

"I try not to think about that," he said. "What if I was healthy and could have achieved what I wanted to and what the Colts wanted me to? I overcame some injuries that were career-[threatening] and played. I didn't let one injury take me out of the game."

Quiet Entrance for Quentin Coryatt

Quentin Coryatt joined the Colts on April 26, 1992, as quietly as possible considering he was the second overall pick in the draft. It was clear from the start the hard-hitting linebacker out of Texas A&M wouldn't exactly be a media darling.

When discussing his selection by the Colts with the Indianapolis media, Coryatt did so on the telephone. But it was hardly a long-distance hookup. Reporters were stationed in the team's locker room. Coryatt was several hundred feet away in the office of general manager Jim Irsay.

"I don't have anything against reporters," insisted the reticent Coryatt. "I just like to do my talking on the field."

Brandon Burlsworth: Tragic Ending

The Burlsworth family was in attendance September 12, 1999. Barbara and her son, Marty, were in the RCA Dome as the Colts opened the regular season with a 31-14 win over Buffalo.

They cheered and wished their son and brother, Brandon, had been able to share the moment. The personable Drew Carey lookalike, complete with the heavy, dark glasses, was there in spirit, in the hearts and minds of the sellout crowd. Brandon Burlsworth had died five months earlier when his car collided with a semi truck in Arkansas.

The Colts' association with Burlsworth was brief. Selected in the third round of the draft, he participated in the team's mini-camp April 24–26. Two days later, while driving to his home in Harrison, Arkansas, after a workout at the University of Arkansas, an accident claimed his life.

The brevity of the team's relationship with Burlsworth couldn't diminish his impact. The Colts affixed a memorial sticker—Burlsworth's "BB" initials inside the team's legendary horseshoe—to each player's helmet for the '99 season. To this day, the Burlsworth Foundation enables youngsters to attend Colts games in Brandon's memory. Look for the "Burls' Kids" banner.

"From everything we could glean, Brandon represented pretty much everything we wanted in a Colt football player," said team president Bill Polian.

Clarence Verdin a Non-Stop Talent

Teammates tagged him CNN because his mouth seemed to be active 24/7. And it didn't matter to Clarence Verdin at whom his diatribes were directed.

During the 1991 preseason, NFL commissioner Paul Tagliabue was in Verdin's verbal crosshairs. The league had instructed its officiating crews to crack down on excessive end zone celebrations during the regular season.

If Verdin was anything, he was excessive. He took Tagliabue's directive personally. Along with running his mouth, Verdin fancied himself as one of the league's premier post-touchdown exhibitionists. His specialty: the Verdance, which was a Michael Jackson–influenced, herky-jerky piece.

"I think they have more important things to worry about," Verdin said, shaking his head. "I was telling a friend of mine that I was going to write Tagliabue and ask if he was going to penalize or fine the fans for doing the wave. The way I look at it, we're entertainers. Fans come to games wanting to be entertained. It's no different than guys slam dunking in basketball. It's showmanship."

Verdin was quite the showman during his six-year career with the Colts. He registered 11 touchdowns—four punt returns, one kickoff return, six receptions—and was voted to the Pro Bowl twice.

Duane Bickett a Reluctant Colt

Long before reality TV gained a foothold in the American culture, there was Duane Bickett, caught on live television, having a difficult time grasping the reality of his situation.

The first round of the 1985 draft was barely an hour old, and the Colts were on the clock with the fifth overall pick. They used it on Bickett, who was convinced he was going to go to Detroit, which was drafting sixth.

"Detroit had called me and said they were going to draft me, welcome to the Lions and this and that," said Bickett.

Instead, it was welcome to Indy. Bickett was surprised, stunned, clearly aggravated by the Colts' decision. He threw up his hands. He uttered an, "Oh, damn." All with a TV camera catching every grimace and grunt.

Blame it on owner Robert Irsay, and blame it on the Colts' unflattering national reputation. In Bickett's mind, any team was a better option than the Colts.

"The reality is that Bob Irsay had a horrible reputation," he said. "John Elway was drafted by them and he refused to play. There was the Frank Kush issue...everything was negative with the Colts.

"It was the unplanned shock, the negativity..."

Soon, Bickett realized his preconceived notion of the Colts was, at least, a case of misinterpreted reality. He stepped into a starting linebacker's role as a rookie and remained a defensive mainstay until he was released after the

1993 season. In 1987, Bickett became the first Colt defender to be selected to the Pro Bowl since 1977. He was the last until defensive end Dwight Freeney was chosen in 2003.

"Once I got there, you realize home is where you are," Bickett said. "It was a great nine years for me."

Sudden Impact by Zack Crockett

You didn't need two hands to tally Zack Crockett's rushing total heading into the 1995 playoffs. Heck, you didn't need two fingers.

The rookie fullback rushed one time for zero yards. That was 1,078 fewer yards than halfback Marshall Faulk's team-leading total.

But when a nagging knee injury flared up on Faulk's first carry against the San Diego Chargers in the first game of the postseason, the Colts put the football, and their fate, in Crockett's hands. He was as ready as a seldom-used backup could be, primarily because director of football operations Bill Tobin, aware of Faulk's fragile knee, put him on alert prior to the game.

"[Tobin] came up to me and said, 'Zack, I need a big day from you.'" Crockett said. "I didn't know it was going to be that big. Everything just opened up. Once I got comfortable back there, it was all she wrote."

The Colts routed the Chargers 35-20 for their first playoff win in 24 years. They followed Crockett's footprints. He rushed 13 times for a club playoff-record 147 yards, including touchdown runs covering 33 and 66 yards.

"When you got your chance," Crockett said, "you had to turn the light on."

Mike Pagel's Fresh Start Short-Lived

The move from Baltimore to Indianapolis in 1984 represented a fresh start for the Colts. And for Mike Pagel.

The team, he believed, was taking serious steps toward respectability, if not the playoffs. And he was its leader, its blue-collar, tough-as-nails quarterback.

"You hated to leave Baltimore because of the longtime tradition," Pagel said. "But at the same time, you had to like the opportunity to go to a brand new city as a young player, especially as a starter, with a team that I thought was on the verge of being a couple of years away from being a serious contender with the young talent we had.

'I thought, 'Wow, what a great opportunity.'"

It didn't last, and neither did Pagel. He started 10 games in 1984 and 14 the following season. In the final game of the '85 season, Pagel enjoyed what he described as "by far my best game as a Colt player." He completed 14 of 22 passes for 178 yards and three touchdowns. The Colts routed Houston 34-16.

A few months later, Pagel was gone, traded to Cleveland for a ninth-round draft pick. His fate was sealed when the Colts, clearly looking for an upgrade at the position, acquired veteran Gary Hogeboom in a trade with Dallas and selected Jack Trudeau in the second round of the draft.

"We were headed in the right direction," said Pagel. "Then a couple of months later...they tell me I'm going to get traded. I was like, 'Thanks a lot, guys.'"

Tony Siragusa Larger than Life

His reputation, one of being unconventional and an unruly free spirit, took firm root at the University of Pittsburgh.

Tony Siragusa's campus companions included a 16-foot boa constrictor, an alligator that dined on rats and a tarantula. He lived life to its fullest. He embraced and maximized every moment.

From 1990–96, Siragusa was the face of the Colts' defense. The "Goose" was stout, rough around the edges, an over-achieving, overweight tackle with bad knees and a bad disposition on game day. He routinely entertained the media and occasionally irritated teammates with his rants and raves in the locker room during the week. But when the time came to get down to business, Siragusa was all business.

"When some people look at a wall, they see a big, flat surface. They don't see what's on the other side," Siragusa said during one of his many philosophical musings. "Well, I'm a person who has other sides. You hear about people with multiple personalities and I guess I'm one of them.

"Sometimes I just want to go home and sit on the couch with my wife and hang out. Other times I want to get on my Harley and go and get crazy."

Chapter Ten

COLTS COACHES

Tony Dungy

Dungy Was "No Doubt" Choice

Tony Dungy was unemployed for eight days, but was there ever a doubt the deposed Tampa Bay Buccaneers coach was headed to Indianapolis?

Not to Jim Irsay. And along with Dungy, his was the opinion that mattered most.

Shortly after Dungy was fired by the Bucs January 14, 2002, following a second straight first-round exit from the playoffs, the Colts' owner reached for his cell phone, punched in the Tampa area code—that's 813—and Dungy's number.

"I just wanted him to know from the start that there was no other coach on the planet I wanted to coach my football team," said Irsay, who was in the market for a coach after firing Jim Mora. "Not [Steve] Spurrier. Not [Bill] Parcells."

The long-distance conversation lasted nearly an hour. If Dungy remained uncertain about the next step, Irsay wasn't. He insisted he was willing to pay top dollar for one of the NFL's top coaches.

Irsay made good on his promise. On January 22, 2002, he signed Dungy to a five-year, $13 million contract.

"You have to pay for greatness," said Irsay. "This was too important a decision for the franchise to not get this done."

Everyone associated with the Colts, along with most national observers, considered it an ideal marriage. The Colts already had a potent offense. What was missing was a reliable defense. Dungy's expertise? Defense.

But Dungy wasn't the first candidate considered to replace Mora. That's because he wasn't available when the Colts began their search.

Once Dungy hit the market, it essentially became a one-man pursuit.

"I knew who I wanted," said Irsay.

Team president Bill Polian called Dungy's hiring "a new beginning."

"The stars came in line for us," said Polian. "That happens sometimes."

Dungy agreed.

"It's the right place at the right time," he said.

More of Moore

If owner Jim Irsay's decision to sign Tony Dungy as head coach was a no-brainer, so was Dungy's decision to retain offensive coordinator Tom Moore.

"I wouldn't be where I am today had it not been for Tom," said Dungy.

Owner Jim Irsay got the coach he wanted when he signed Tony Dungy in January 2002. (Rob Goebel/*The Indianapolis Star*)

It was Moore, an assistant coach at the University of Minnesota in 1972, who recruited Dungy out of high school and helped him evolve into a record-setting quarterback for the Golden Gophers. It was Moore, as one of Chuck Noll's assistants, who convinced the Pittsburgh Steelers to sign Dungy as an undrafted free agent in 1977.

In 1992–93, Moore and Dungy served on Dennis Green's staff with the Minnesota Vikings. Twice during his six-year stint as head coach in Tampa, Dungy attempted to hire Moore as his offensive coordinator. On each occasion, Moore was under contract and unavailable.

Then Dungy relocated to Indianapolis and finally was reunited with Moore.

"It's funny how the Lord works things out," said Dungy. "We had always talked about coaching back together again. And for me to come to a place where he already was just makes it so much more comfortable for me.

"He's probably like an older brother."

Nice Combination

A wrinkle would creep across quarterback Peyton Manning's forehead every time someone implied Tony Dungy is more interested in the defensive workings of the Colts than with how one of the NFL's most potent offenses operates.

Dungy's coaching background certainly was rooted on the defensive side of the line of scrimmage. But he didn't require a map when he stepped to the other side.

"Tony's in our meetings all the time. I believe he's in our offensive meetings more than he is in the defensive meetings," said Manning. "He sits in the back. He chimes in. He's very vocal. You hear the door close and he's back with the defense, but a little later he comes back to our meeting."

Dungy was a record-setting quarterback at the University of Minnesota. Upon graduation in 1976, he owned school career passing records for attempts (576), completions (274), yards (3,577) and touchdowns (25). He was named the Golden Gophers' Most Valuable Player twice and ranked fourth in Big Ten history in total offense behind Mike Phipps, Archie Griffin and Bob Griese.

So when Dungy offered advice, Manning generally heeded it. He understood it was the voice with experience on each side of the ball.

"I always thought a defensive coordinator was a great guy to talk with," said Manning. "I wish I had time to sit in on some defensive meetings to listen to how they approach things. 'Why does this play work or what should this guy have done?'

"With Tony, I'm getting some of that. He'll say, 'Hey, this play would be good. Hey, on this play, if this receiver did this, it would be even better.' That's going to help me out.

"I never bought into the idea Tony was only here to help out our defense. Tony isn't calling our defense. [Coordinator] Ron Meeks is calling the defense. Tony is the head coach and he's in charge of the whole team."

Better Second Time Around

The first time Tony Dungy slipped into the head coaching seat, it took his Tampa Bay Buccaneers six games to deliver a victory.

The Colts didn't test his patience in 2002. Dungy made it clear during a team meeting several months before the September 8 opener at Jacksonville that he wasn't interested in overseeing a long-range rebuilding project.

"He said he's not here to help us win next year or two years from now," said Manning. "He wants to win this year."

The Colts obliged, launching the Dungy era with a 28-25 victory over the Jaguars.

"I'm just glad I got it. It took me a little longer the first time," said Dungy.

In 1996, Dungy's first year as a head coach, the Bucs dropped their first five games before presenting him his first career victory, a 24-13 decision over Minnesota.

His Calming Influence

Jon Gruden gave the Chucky glare. Bill Cowher stuck out his squared jaw. Some coaches rant, rave and do a slow but detectable burn.

Tony Dungy? On the sideline, he was generally poise personified; arms crossed, little hint of emotion that might convey whether his team's up 14 or trailing by 10. During a losing streak, he was composed, unflustered, in control of himself and his team.

"For us, his greatest strength was how he dealt with adversity," said Rich McKay, who worked with Dungy for six years as Tampa Bay's general manager. "In this league, you're facing adversity on a yearly basis at some point in time. You'll hear the comment 'a calming force,' but it's a quiet confidence. You know with him that he remains confident and remains very dedicated to the plan."

Not Always Mr. Nice Guy

Tony Dungy was known for his sideline decorum. He was poised, pleasant. Most of the time. But not with 42 seconds remaining in the second quarter of a 2003 game at New Orleans.

Dungy was irritated when Saints running back Deuce McAllister scored on a one-yard run with very little resistance. Contributing to the easy score was improper goal line alignment by the Colts' defense. TV cameras caught Dungy dressing down his defense.

"He doesn't get mad very often," said veteran Chad Bratzke, "so when he gets mad, you can hear a pin drop."

"Players listen because Dungy picks his spot. He just doesn't bark to hear himself bark.

"When you have a dog that just barks constantly, pretty soon you don't hear that dog barking any more. When he doesn't bark very often and you hear some barking, that gets your attention."

Keeping His Priorities Straight

Anyone who questioned Tony Dungy's head coaching acumen hadn't been paying attention. In eight seasons, he posted an 80-58 record and reached the playoffs six times. In 1999, he guided Tampa Bay to the NFC title game. In '03, he directed the Colts to the AFC title game.

Winning football games, though, hardly defined Dungy. Ask him to rank his priorities, and football comes in third behind faith and family.

His personal resume includes associations with Fellowship of Christian Athletes, Boys and Girls Club and Family First, a non-profit agency devoted to strengthening family values. He and Clyde Christensen, his offensive coordinator in Tampa and receivers coach with the Colts, launched All-Pro Dads, which champions fatherhood. On occasion, Dungy has taken his message of faith and hope to prisons.

Coaching in the NFL was Dungy's vocation and an opportunity to do so much more. As one of only five African American head coaches, he was infinitely visible and always eager to maximize his built-in platform. He's a member of the Fritz Pollard Alliance, which was formed to further minority causes in the NFL.

Perspective from the Young

The cruel finality of the end of his first season with the Colts hardly had time to set in. The New York Jets still were celebrating their 41-0 2002 first-round playoff rout at Giants Stadium.

Tony Dungy was heading off the field when perspective tugged at his sleeve. Eric, one of his three sons who routinely works as a ball boy on game day, had a request that demanded an immediate response.

"We had just lost 41-nothing and he looked at me and said, 'Dad, I know we lost and I know it wasn't a good game, but can I go over and meet [Jets' receiver] Santana Moss?'" Dungy said.

"That kind of put it all in perspective. There are a lot of people who really don't care."

Practice Makes Perfect

Tony Dungy isn't one to stand idly by and watch practice unfold. When the time came for the Peyton Manning–led No. 1 offense to work against the "scout defense," Dungy frequently stepped in to run the unit that mirrored the upcoming opponent. It's a coaching technique he adopted during his days as Dennis Green's defensive coordinator with the Minnesota Vikings.

Rather than have the scout defense simply follow a scripted game plan, Dungy occasionally called an audible to test Manning's ability to adjust at the line of scrimmage.

"He might call a blitz that we haven't seen," said Manning. "I might say, 'They don't do that.' He says, 'Well, guess what? They could.'"

Back from the Dead

He'll never be mistaken for Chris Rock, Dennis Miller or some other stand-up comedian. But occasionally, Tony Dungy is good for a laugh.

Take the Colts' 35-13 rout of the Philadelphia Eagles at Veterans Stadium on November 10, 2002. It was Dungy's first visit to the Vet in 10 months. On January 12, his Tampa Bay Buccaneers were dealt a 31-9 loss that resulted in a second straight first-round playoff exit. Shortly thereafter, Dungy was fired.

As he prepared to meet the media after the Colts' convincing victory, Dungy paused, and smiled.

"I have to laugh because 10 months ago, I guess, I was here right behind this podium and everybody thought I was dead," Dungy said.

Cuts Tough on Everybody

Cuts are as inevitable as fumbles, but that doesn't mean Tony Dungy has to like them any better. He is too sensitive to the players' feelings. He recalls too well his own feelings. He recalls his third year in Pittsburgh, 1979.

"We were still at training camp and it was real late, right before we were getting ready for the team meeting," said Dungy. "I was sitting in Joe Greene's room; there was Joe Greene, Mel Blount, myself and Franco Harris. We were sitting there saying, 'This is taking a long time. There's got to be somebody that nobody can figure out. This is taking too long; normally it's done by now.'

"So a guy came down and knocked on the door. I knew they weren't knocking for Joe or Franco or Mel. That was my day out."

Dungy didn't get cut. He was traded to San Francisco for a 10th-round draft pick. The following season, he was traded to the New York Giants for Ray Rhodes. As Dungy said, "That got both of us into coaching." Both players were cut.

Nor is the anxiety always on the side of the player, another lesson Dungy learned at Pittsburgh. In 1978, the Steelers traded defensive tackle Ernie Holmes, a notorious tough guy, to Tampa Bay.

"No one wanted to tell him," said Dungy. "We couldn't get any volunteers. I don't know how he actually found out, but nobody wanted to be the one to make that call."

There's a kicker to the story. Pittsburgh used the 1980 10th-round pick it received for Dungy to draft North Carolina State cornerback Woodrow Wilson, who proved more presidential in name than performance.

Wilson was cut during training camp.

Jim Mora

A Second Chance

One minute, Jim Mora was sharing breakfast with Connie, his wife of 38 years, at the couple's condominium in San

Diego. The next, he was returning to the NFL as the head coach of the Colts.

It had been nearly 15 months since Mora, emotional and spent, walked away from the New Orleans Saints midway through the 1996 season. He needed a break, and he gave himself one. He needed new direction, and he found it as an analyst for NBC's NFL broadcasts.

Jim Mora was the passionate leader of the Colts until he refused to fire his defensive coordinator. (Steve Healey/*The Indianapolis Star*)

Then, as January 8, 1998, was dawning in the Mora household, the telephone rang. Colts president Bill Polian was at the other end, offering Mora an opportunity to resuscitate his coaching career.

Connie recalled a conversation she had with her husband the night before Polian shook up their world. "We looked at each other and said, 'We're not ready to be retired.' We really like working," she said. "Playing golf for the rest of your life, I look around and go, 'This is really fun, but what are you going to do?'

"And then [the next morning], there was that call. It dropped right out of heaven. When something like that happens, you just know it's right."

The timing, insisted Mora, was perfect. He liked broadcasting, but still was distressed by the manner in which his stint with the Saints ended.

"I didn't want to end my career that way," he said. "I believe I've got a second chance here. I'm humbled and appreciative to have that second chance, and I'm going to bust my butt to help this team win."

Too Good, Too Soon

The Colts were too good, too soon for Jim Mora's own good. He inherited a team that finished a league-worst 3-13 in 1997, and guided it to an identical record in his first season. But in '99, the Mora-led Colts went from worst to first—a 13-3 record and the AFC East title.

That not only established the biggest one-season turnaround in NFL history, it also established unrealistic expectations. The Colts earned their second straight playoff berth under Mora in 2000, but it was a struggle. It took a season-ending three-game winning streak for them to post a 10-6 record and secure a wild card berth. The 2001 season was sabotaged by injuries, most notably a season-ending knee injury to running back Edgerrin James, and an ineffective defense. The Colts finished 6-10, and Mora was fired when he refused to dismiss defensive coordinator Vic Fangio.

Mora likened his ability to transform the Colts from afterthoughts to playoff participants to his career with the New Orleans Saints. At each stop, he was too good, too soon.

"You know what mistake we made down there?" he asked.

"We won too quickly. You come into a team that's been losing, you should go 6-10, 7-9, 9-7. Then when they're ready to fire you, you go 11-5."

Mr. Emotional

They were called Mora Moments, snippets of temper or raw emotion that bubbled to the surface and found themselves forever engrained in the psyche of football fans and ESPN.

Who can forget Jim Mora's tearful farewell to New Orleans? One day he's blasting the underachieving, 2-6 Saints along with the coaches and himself. The next day, he resigns.

Mora admitted he learned his lesson from that humbling "meltdown." Hardly mellow, he at least was more in control during his four years in Indy. Most of the time.

There was that August afternoon in '99 when the Colts were wrapping up training camp in Terre Haute. Already irritated by a sloppy practice, Mora noticed wide receiver Jerome Pathon sitting on his helmet as he watched a drill that didn't include him. "The next guy I see sitting on his helmet is out of here," Mora snapped. "I don't give a damn who it is."

And his response to a reporter's question after a November 25, 2001, loss to San Francisco that dropped the Colts' record to 4-6. Does the team, the reporter asked, still have a shot at making the playoffs?

"Playoffs? Don't talk about playoffs. Are you kidding me? Playoffs?" snapped Mora. "I just hope we can win a game, another game."

Finally, the moments after the Colts closed the 2001 season with a 29-10 victory over Denver. The majority of his postgame press conference focused on his future. It seemed inevitable that he would be fired in the coming days.

"You appear very emotional," a reporter asked. "A lot of feelings inside?"

"Whooaaa," Mora said, choking up. "Yeah."

There was a sniffle. Then Mora turned around and slammed his hand against the backdrop behind the podium.

"A lot of them," he said.

He continued to struggle for his composure.

"I'm sorry."

After gaining his composure, Mora defended his body of work and that of his coaching staff. He did so with gusto.

"Am I emotional? Damn right I'm emotional," he said. "And I apologize."

Loyal to the End

Jim Mora could have saved his job, finished out the five-year contract he signed in 1998. But the cost was too high.

The Colts' defense allowed points in waves during the 2001 regular season, 486 in all, the fourth highest total in NFL history. If Mora was to return for 2002, it would be without Vic Fangio, his defensive coordinator and, more important, his friend.

"I was asked by Bill Polian to fire Vic Fangio and I wouldn't do it," said Mora.

Fangio would not have left the Colts and spent any time in the unemployment line. He already was in line to become the defensive coordinator of the expansion Houston Texans. But Mora stood by his convictions. He stood by Vic. And it got him fired.

"It's about what's right and what's wrong," said Mora. "It's that simple."

Ted Marchibroda

Thanks, See Ya

Ted Marchibroda's second stint with the Colts ended in January 1996 amid controversy and with a handshake.

Less than a week after directing the franchise to its first AFC championship game in 24 years, Marchibroda was fired by director of football operations Bill Tobin.

"I talked briefly with Bill and he said they were going in another direction," Marchibroda said. "I shook his hand, and that was the extent of the conversation."

Marchibroda was under contract through the 1996 season and sought an extension. Tobin offered a one-year extension with a modest pay raise. When Marchibroda balked, Tobin pulled the trigger.

"I'm a free agent," Marchibroda said.

Firing a coach wasn't exactly a rarity for the Colts. Marchibroda was the team's sixth head coach or interim coach since their relocation to Indianapolis.

Ted Marchibroda directed the Colts to the '95 AFC title game, then became "a free agent." (Patrick Schneider/*The Indianapolis Star*)

But Marchibroda's release wasn't popular. In an informal telephone poll taken by *The Indianapolis Star* immediately after the firing, 4,346 of 4,713 respondents (92 percent) believed the Colts had treated Marchibroda unfairly.

Marchibroda remains tied with Hall of Famer Don Shula as the winningest coach in Colts history. He posted a 73-71 record while coaching the team from 1975–79 and 1992–95. Marchibroda's resume includes four playoff appearances, capped by the 20-16 loss to Pittsburgh in the AFC title game after the '95 regular season.

In 2002, he was included in the team's Ring of Honor at the RCA Dome, joining late owner Robert Irsay, Bill Brooks and Chris Hinton.

Fondest Farewell

The Colts gave Ted Marchibroda a going-away present that remains one of his most indelible memories: A loss.

After four quarters of trading haymakers with Pittsburgh in the AFC championship game after the 1995 season, the Colts were four points short. They lost 20-16, ending a dramatic playoff run and, as fate would have it, Marchibroda's second tour of duty with the franchise.

But as he addressed his players in the locker room at Three Rivers Stadium, Marchibroda knew he was surrounded by a special group. Losers? Only on the scoreboard.

"Without question, the most powerful locker room I've ever been associated with was after the Pittsburgh loss," said Marchibroda. "You saw the faces of the guys, the whole locker room. The energy, the electricity, the intensity.

"They had given everything they had. There was no more to give, and it had to end like that. There was disappointment, and yet there was joy, too. They knew what they had accomplished."

Lindy Infante

The inevitable would occur six weeks later, when the Colts would begin the search for their sixth head coach in 15 seasons. But for one escapist afternoon, everything was right in Lindy Infante's world.

Virtually everyone expected the 11th game of the 1997 regular season to mirror the previous 10, all of which were losses. On hand to extend the Colts' futility and push Infante closer to the firing line were the defending Super Bowl champion Green Bay Packers.

"I could stand here and say it's just another football game, but I'm human," said Infante, the Packers' head coach from 1988–91. "I'd be lying if I said this wasn't especially gratifying."

"This" was a stunning 41-38 upset of Green Bay.

In the days leading up to the game, Infante used the aura of the Packers as motivation. They were the measuring stick for excellence.

"...what a great opportunity this was to prove to the world we weren't near as bad as our record," said the embattled Infante. "The best way to prove that was to beat the world champions."

Quarterback Paul Justin passed for a career-high 340 yards and one touchdown. Running back Marshall Faulk carved out 116 yards on 17 rushing attempts. Tight end Ken Dilger caught six passes for 96 yards, and it was his 28-yard catch-and-run with less than two minutes to play in a 38-all game that produced a first and goal at the Green Bay one.

After three kneel-downs by Justin, placekicker Cary Blanchard completed the shocker with a 20-yard field goal.

While exhilarating, the victory was little more than a rest stop on the road to nowhere. The Colts lost their next two games and three of their final five. The day after a season-ending 39-28 loss at Minnesota, Infante and Bill Tobin, the team's director of football operations, were fired.

"I appreciate the opportunity I was given, but it just didn't work out," said Infante, who had directed the Colts to a 9-7 record and a playoff berth in '96 before things regressed to a 3-13 finish in '97.

Ron Meyer

Slick salesman or savvy coach? You make the call.

Owner Robert Irsay was in search of the latter when he fired Rod Dowhower 13 games—13 losses—into the 1986 season. He called Ron Meyer.

"I don't envision myself as a Messiah or a genius," Meyer said. "Obviously, we're facing an uphill battle."

Perhaps it took someone of Meyer's ilk to breathe life into a moribund franchise. Prior to his arrival on December 1, 1986, and since their relocation to Indianapolis in 1984, the Colts had won nine of 45 games. Their 13-game losing streak to open the '86 season was the worst start in the history of a franchise that was all too familiar with long losing streaks.

Meyer talked a good game. When he was head coach at Southern Methodist, Dallas reporters called him the "Pro of Con." During his stint at coach of the New England Patriots, a portion of the media referred to him as a used car salesman.

Nothing wrong with that, insisted Meyer. His father was a salesman.

"I've heard that description of myself and I don't consider myself a super salesman," he said. "But, honestly, aren't we all salesmen? Aren't we all selling a product, a service or ourselves?"

Meyer was quick-witted, engaging, a master motivator. Teams responded to his charisma. He turned around college football programs at the University of Nevada-Las Vegas and SMU. He turned around the Patriots. And, given his second NFL head coaching job by Irsay, he turned around the Colts.

They won their first three games with Meyer bouncing confidently on the sideline. The 13-game losing streak ended in rousing fashion as a blocked punt by safety Tate Randle and a goal-line stand in the closing seconds contributed to a 28-23 win at Atlanta.

"Luckier than a blind dog in a meat house," the folksy Meyer said of the victory over the Falcons.

Rod Dowhower

It's safe to say two issues led to the dismissal of coach Rod Dowhower 13 games into the 1986 season.

First, his Colts were 0-13 and giving every indication they were headed to 0-16.

Second, his relationship with owner Robert Irsay had deteriorated so much that the franchise's two main figures barely spoke.

The end came on December 1. Out went Dowhower and his 5-24 record, worst among NFL active coaches at the time. In came Meyer, who was on the verge of being named the head coach at Purdue University before Irsay decided enough was enough and fired Dowhower.

Despite the Colts' horrendous start, Irsay steadfastly insisted he would wait until the end of the season before evaluating Dowhower. Injuries had sabotaged the team almost from the outset. Starting quarterback Gary Hogeboom suffered a separated shoulder in the second game of the season, forcing rookie Jack Trudeau into the starting lineup. All told, front-line players missed a combined 73 games because of injuries during the 13-game losing streak.

Irsay's patience, though, was gone after the Colts' 17-3 loss to the San Diego Chargers in the Hoosier Dome. Asked about Dowhower's status in the aftermath of loss No. 13, Irsay replied: "We go hour to hour, day to day, week to week."

The players sensed a change was imminent prior to the Chargers game. Several said Dowhower stopped to shake hands with them prior to kickoff, a routine he had not previously followed.

Dowhower offered no excuses after his dismissal. "If you could put your finger on one thing and say *that* is the reason, it would be easy," he said. "But I guess I'm the easy way out."

But it wasn't an easy out for either Dowhower or Irsay.

Although Dowhower's salary was guaranteed through the '87 season, Irsay refused to honor his former coach's contract. Irsay insisted Dowhower breached the contract by failing to communicate with him on a regular basis. Dowhower filed a grievance with the NFL, which ruled in his favor.

Frank Kush

The first NFL head coach the city of Indianapolis knew failed to reach the finish line in his first season. Frank Kush resigned with one game remaining in the 1984 regular season.

He returned to his home in Tempe, Arizona, and was named head coach of the USFL's Arizona Outlaws. That league dissolved after the 1985 season, leaving Kush without a coaching job but with no regrets.

"Making that decision was like coming to a 'Y' in the road," Kush said of leaving the Colts after three seasons. "I evaluated both sides and realized that Arizona, a place I really love, was where I wanted to be.

"I also loved the people of Indianapolis, but I felt the USFL had a good chance. And at my age, it provided the kind of financial security I needed for myself and my family."

In three seasons with the Colts, Kush led the team to an 11-28-1 record.

Humble Beginnings to Canton

Tony Dungy's path to Canton, Ohio, home of the Pro Football Hall of Fame, weaved through Pittsburgh, San Francisco, Kansas City, Minneapolis, Tampa and Indianapolis. It involved a short stint as a player with the Steelers and 49ers, and assistant coaching stints with the Steelers, Chiefs and Vikings. But it blossomed as a transcendent head coach with the Buccaneers and Colts.

He remained humble and appreciative throughout the journey. A quiet wit was a constant companion, and was present on the Hall of Fame stage August 6, 2016, when Dungy offered his acceptance speech.

"I'm now the tenth Steeler from the Super Bowl 13 team to be enshrined," he said. "But you could have won a lot of money in '78 if you had bet that I would be one of those 10.

"I remember making a tackle my rookie year and Dwight White asking in the huddle, 'What's your name again? How are you still on the team?' So it really is kind of a miracle that I'm here and I'm thrilled to have my Steeler roommate and should-be-Hall of Famer, Donnie Shell, presenting me."

Dungy's addition to the Pro Football Hall of Fame was hardly a miracle. It was the byproduct of more than three decades in the NFL as a player, assistant coach, defensive coordinator and head coach. He retired after the 2008 season, ending 13 seasons as a head coach, the final seven with the Colts.

His resume in Indy was fat. He remains the winningest coach in team history (92-33 including the playoffs). The Colts won at least 10 games and reached the postseason in each of his seven seasons, and set an NFL record by winning at least 12 games in six consecutive seasons. Including his time with the Bucs, Dungy set an NFL record by taking a team to the playoffs in 10 consecutive seasons.

The capper came February 4, 2007, when the Colts defeated the Chicago Bears 29-17 in Super Bowl XLI and Dungy became the first African-American head coach to win a Super Bowl.

"I've never seen the type of leadership, the type of head coaching abilities that Tony brings," Colts owner Jim Irsay said. "Obviously being the first African-American (coach) to win a Super Bowl, that speaks for itself.

"What he means to the game . . . there's a reverence around him. He always leaves a legacy for the Horseshoe."

Dungy cherished his time in Indianapolis. He was added to the Colts' Ring of Honor in 2010.

"It was a tremendous time in my life and some great people," he said. "I really have to look at the Lord just guiding me there. I got fired in Tampa and you don't know what's going to happen and where you're going to go or if you're going to go anywhere.

"I have to thank my boss. Jim Irsay gave me a call, left a message on my answering machine. He said, 'We want to build a team the right way in Indianapolis. We want to connect with our fans and have a team that represents our city well.' Didn't talk about championships or any of that. Just talked about how he wanted to do it and he said, 'You're the guy I want to lead us.'"

Chapter Eleven

ETC., PART 1

Death of Robert Irsay

Robert Irsay could be controversial and cantankerous, calculated and callous. He meddled when he shouldn't have, fired coaches at the drop of a hat.

Asked once on by an Indianapolis television reporter how much football he knew, Irsay replied, "Just enough to be dangerous."

But he also could be charitable and entertaining. Loathed in Baltimore for robbing the city of the Colts in 1984, he was embraced by Indianapolis. An estimated 20,000 fans filed into the Hoosier Dome on March 30, 1984, to welcome him and his NFL franchise.

On January 14, 1997, Irsay died at Indiana University Hospital, more than two years after suffering a serious stroke.

Approximately 400 people gathered at St. Luke Catholic Church for Irsay's memorial service. NFL commissioner Paul Tagliabue attended. So did Frank Kush, the head coach Irsay brought with him from Baltimore, and Ted Marchibroda, who twice served as Irsay's head coach.

"I had a great respect for him," said Kush. "He and I are from the same kind of background—the work ethic, the discipline. That's why we got along."

Added Marchibroda: "He was a hard man to get to know, but once you got to know him, you had to like him. In my estimation, Bob Irsay was a very good man."

It was cruel irony that Irsay was unable to enjoy one of his franchise's greatest moments. A late-season push enabled the Colts to earn a wild card playoff berth in 1995. In the post-season, they went on the road and upset San Diego and Kansas City before losing at Pittsburgh in the AFC championship game.

The magical playoff run unfolded as Irsay fought for his life. He suffered a stroke in November of '95.

Jim Irsay Overcomes Addiction

The most important member of the Colts' organization acknowledged in 2002 that he had addressed a most personal and pressing problem.

Owner Jim Irsay admitted that he sought treatment for an addiction to prescription pain medication. Although he avoided talking publicly about his problem, Irsay said in a statement: "After several years of orthopedic operations and procedures, accompanied by long bouts of chronic pain, I became dependent on prescription pain medication. This summer I sought professional help at a nationally recognized facility located outside Indiana. I have successfully dealt with my dependence and my chronic pain issues."

No Johnny U. Tribute

Call it the Great Shoe Debate. And throw a flag at the NFL for unnecessary enforcement.

It was Peyton Manning's wish to pay tribute to Johnny Unitas, the former Baltimore Colts quarterback who died September 11, 2002, by wearing a pair of black hightops—Unitas's trademark footwear—in a September 15 game against Miami. Because of the sensitive nature of the gesture, Manning checked with one of Unitas's sons, Joe. He was told the family thought wearing the black hightops would be an appropriate tribute.

The NFL, which is stickler on uniform conformity and reluctant to allow individual tributes, thought otherwise.

"They said there would be a horrendous fine if I did," said Manning.

So he didn't.

"Somebody has passed away and the one thing I didn't want to do was create a controversy," said Manning, who wore black hightops at the University of Tennessee to honor the Hall of Fame QB.

Tobin vs. Kiper

Long before the great Bill Polian–Jay Mohr radio debate and Jim Mora's indelible assessment of a 2001 season gone bad—*"Playoff...playoffs??"*—there were Bill Tobin and Mel Kiper, Jr.

And there were verbal fireworks ignited by Kiper's criticism of the Colts' decision to use the fifth overall pick in the 1994 draft on Nebraska linebacker Trev Alberts and not

Fresno State quarterback Trent Dilfer. The Colts had selected San Diego State running back Marshall Faulk with the second overall pick.

Kiper, a draft analyst with ESPN, felt the Colts' most pressing need was a quarterback. At the time, the team's QB of choice was Jim Harbaugh.

"To me, this was a mistake," said Kiper. "You cannot go with Jim Harbaugh and pass up Trent Dilfer. Forget it. That's why the Colts are the laughingstock of the league year-in and year-out."

Tobin, the Colts' director of football operations, took exception to the comments, then took on Kiper.

"Who the hell is Mel Kiper anyway?" he asked. "He didn't play college or pro football. I don't know about high school, and to my knowledge he's never put on a jock strap, so all of a sudden he's an expert?

"Mel Kiper has no more credentials to do what he's doing than my neighbor, and my neighbor's a postman."

In retrospect, chalk this one up for Tobin.

With Faulk positioned behind him, Harbaugh was more than good enough. "Captain Comeback" directed the Colts to consecutive playoff appearances in 1995–96. The highlight was a trip to the AFC championship game after the '95 regular season.

Dilfer? Taken sixth overall by Tampa Bay in '94, he helped lead the Buccaneers to two playoff appearances in six seasons. His crowning achievement, though, occurred with Baltimore in 2000 when he was part of the Ravens' Super Bowl championship squad. Some were convinced Dilfer was just along for the ride. The Ravens' defense, led by manic linebacker Ray Lewis, was smothering, stifling.

First Pick a Late Arrival

The Colts got their man, albeit later than anticipated.

Sixteen months after making Vanderbilt cornerback Leonard Coleman the eighth overall pick in the 1984 draft and the first ever pick of the Indy era, the team got his name on a contract.

"This is where I want to play," said Coleman.

That was September 18, 1985. The previous year, Coleman wanted no part of the Colts or their four-year contract offer that was valued at approximately $1.7 million. Unable to squeeze more money out of general manager Jim Irsay, Coleman signed a four-year, $2 million deal with the Memphis Showboats of the United States Football League.

Coleman's fascination with Memphis and the USFL quickly waned. With the rival league on shaky financial ground, players began looking for avenues that led them to the NFL. Coleman was the sixth member of the Showboats to jump ship. A seventh would soon follow—defensive end Reggie White, destined for NFL greatness, initially with the Philadelphia Eagles.

Although the Colts inserted Coleman into their secondary, he never came close to fulfilling expectations. He was gone after three nondescript seasons. His legacy: four career interceptions, all in 1986 with three coming against the New Orleans Saints.

Determination Is in His Genes

David Thornton arrived at the University of North Carolina as a 170-pound "uninvited" walk-on. He departed a 225-pound linebacker and a fourth-round draft pick who had been voted the Tar Heels' defensive MVP over teammates Julius Peppers and Ryan Sims, a defensive end and tackle who were among the first six players taken in the 2002 draft.

That kind of journey requires a singular depth of determination, and one needn't look far to find its source. Thornton's father, Arnold, is a Pentecostal minister whose ministry takes him to prisons all over North Carolina. Arnold Thornton connects with the inmates he serves. Much of his life was lost to drugs and hard knocks.

"I ended up with a needle in my arm. From 1957 to 1972, I used drugs, I robbed stores, broke in, you name it, I did it," said Arnold. "I was in and out of jail. Nothing but the mercy of God saved me."

Arnold found God's mercy in 1973. He had hit rock bottom. People told him he would die there. He turned his life over to the Lord and went cold turkey.

"The more they told me I couldn't do it, the more determined I was to live my life for Christ," he said. "I look at David as having that same zeal for whatever he wanted to do. He always gave it his best."

David is a deeply spiritual yes-sir, no-sir kind of guy who in his first season as a starter led the Colts with 158 tackles. He has just kept improving.

"There were definitely some tough times in the midst of it all," he said, "but I never thought about quitting."

Singing His Praises

Visit Livermore, Iowa, a smattering of houses amidst the gently rolling cornfields of the north plains country and you will find no stoplights and 431 residents. All of them, it seems, are anxious to talk about Dallas Clark.

Family, friends, neighbors, teachers, they all say the same kinds of things about the Twin River Valley's favorite son. An image emerges. Family friend Greg Lemke even enunciated it:

"He's a choir boy."

That's a fact corroborated by Denise Foth. She taught Clark in elementary school. She was music director of the United Methodist Church youth choir.

"He had to sing a solo once," said Foth. "He didn't come in quite right, and all the boys kind of got the giggles."

It's Humboldt County residents doing the singing now. They sing Clark's praises. He was a University of Iowa walk-on who in 2002 won the John Mackey Award presented annually to college football's premiere tight end, and in 2003 he became the Colts' first-round draft choice.

Clark's aw-shucks manner won friends in the locker room and fans in the stands, but his big impact was restoring some bite to the Colts' two–tight end set with Marcus Pollard. Clark flashed his bright potential by catching 29 passes for 340 yards and one touchdown despite missing six games with injuries.

A Brace of Hawkeyes

The Colts made it two for two in April 2004, when for the second successive year, they went to Iowa with their first pick in the draft. It was Dallas Clark with the 24th selection of the first round in 2003 and 5'8" mighty-mite safety Bob Sanders at No. 44 after the club traded down to the second round in 2004.

According to Hawkeyes coach Kirk Ferentz, Clark and Sanders have more in common than their alma mater and their current working address.

"[Kirk] told me, 'Last year you got the guy that energized our whole team on offense,'" Colts president Bill Polian said. "'This year you got the guy who energized our defense.'"

Sanders has exceptional 4.35-second speed and an inexhaustible well of energy. As a youth, his father Marion said, Bob ran everywhere. Into the house. Out of the house. He ran while he played. He ran while he worked. He ran to the bathroom. He ran to dinner. He ran not to bed, but from it.

"He fell asleep one night and got up at 9 or 10 and headed for the door," recalled Marion. "I followed him outside and he started running; I don't know where he was going, maybe his friend's.

"He was probably six years old, but he got 50 yards ahead of me. He ran three or four blocks and I couldn't catch him. He sleep-ran."

Bowling for Dollars

You want hip? Wide receiver Reggie Wayne is hip. Running back Edgerrin James is hip. So is defensive end Dwight Freeney.

So what do they enjoy during a night out? Bowling. Cool is as cool does.

"It's cool for me," said Wayne. "I'll take bowling over anything. I'll take bowling over video games."

Wayne and quarterback Peyton Manning have held charity bowling tournaments, during which the players bowl as teams, but if you want the real get-down, come to south Florida in the summertime. Miami residents James and Wayne, Tennessee cornerback Samari Rolle, Green Bay tight end Bubba Franks and New York Jets wide receiver Santana Moss get together and bowl all night.

"It's cool when you're gambling," James said with his wide, gold-toothed grin. "We only bet $10, $20, but it's the competition. You stand there all hours. We pay the people to keep the lanes open until six, seven in the morning."

Wayne doesn't need the monetary incentive. He just loves bowling. He watches it on ESPN. When he can stir no interest, he sometimes goes to an alley alone. He averages 190 to 200.

Said Wayne, "I break a sweat bowling."

Wayne Blossoms After Finding His Slot

Reggie Wayne was not a burner. But he was a sure-handed 203-pound wide receiver who probably was the Colts' best player at running after the catch, and in 2002, he found a home. Wayne made a living playing the slot.

He lined up a step off the line of scrimmage, between the tight end and the split end. His area of operations was primarily over the middle, an area dominated by high-speed traffic and high-impact collisions.

"You'd better bring your hard hat," said Wayne.

Wayne wasn't initially enthusiastic about working there. He regarded it as the domain of the small, quick receiver, the Troy Walters type, but mostly he wanted to play. He wanted to catch passes. He knew he was an unpopular pick when he was chosen 30th overall in the 2001 draft.

Colts fans wanted a run-stuffing tackle or a pass-rushing end.

So he devoted his summer after the 2001 season to preparation.

"I went out with the mind frame that I had to prove to everybody that I was a good pick, that I wasn't a bust," he said.

"That was my whole focus all summer."

He caught 49 passes for 716 yards and four touchdowns in 2002. He had 68 catches for 838 yards and seven touchdowns in 2003. Again and again, he was a productive target on third down.

Wayne, with Marvin Harrison and Brandon Stokley or Walters, became a crucial connection in a three–wide receiver set that was one of the NFL's best.

"Reggie has learned to be patient, that I'll come to him," said quarterback Peyton Manning. "I wouldn't trade our three guys for anybody."

A Big Pop, and a Bit of Payback

Rookie safety Mike Doss made one of the more memorable hits of the Colts' 2003 season.

On a third-quarter run during a September game at the RCA Dome, Jacksonville running back Fred Taylor blasted up the middle, then angled toward the left sideline. David Thornton took Taylor low. Doss roared out of the secondary like a 207-pound guided missile and blasted Taylor high.

The football popped loose, and while Colts safety Idrees Bashir covered it, Doss lingered over Taylor.

"You lost something," he chided.

Taylor heard, and remembered.

"I told one of your media outlets I was going to bust his [butt] next game," Taylor said the week of the AFC South members' November rematch. "I don't mind if you guys tell him that, and I'm sticking to that."

Doss smiled when informed of Taylor's comments after practice that day.

"I'm definitely looking forward to the matchup," he said. "He's a good running back, but I've got a job to do. I'm not backing down, not at all."

Give Round 1 to the rookie safety. Give Round 2 to the veteran running back.

Taylor ran for 152 yards and two touchdowns as the Jaguars upset the Colts, 28-23, in Jacksonville. Personal payback came with just over a minute remaining. On his game-deciding 32-yard touchdown, Taylor burst through the heart of the Colts' defense and ran through Doss's tackle.

"He got the last word right there," said Doss. "When a safety misses a tackle, it's a touchdown. It was me against Fred Taylor."

"We're even now," replied Taylor.

Talk Not Always Cheap

Left tackle Tarik Glenn has a degree in social welfare from the University of California and a philosophy of life his studies helped form. Just ask him. Then again, don't. Glenn is a man of conviction and an inclination to share his views.

Teammates referred to insightful offensive tackle Tarik Glenn as "Taristotle." (Rob Goebel/*The Indianapolis Star****)***

"We try not to get into politics or government, but Tarik likes it when it gets a little hot in that [offensive line meeting] room," said Adam Meadows, who played tackle for the Colts from 1997 through 2003. "He likes to talk about anything, but especially football, and he'll give you a dissertation on what he thinks and why."

Glenn became such an expansive philosopher, such a fervent orator, that his linemates distinguished him with a name. "Taristotle" they called him, or alternately, "Tariklete."

That doesn't mean they always accorded one of the most respected Colts full respect. The offensive line is a team within the team. It has its own system of justice, one that features an extensive structure of fines and can tend toward the arbitrary.

"Any time he starts going into a dissertation, we just cut him off," said Meadows. "We fine him."

Chatter isn't the only violation that results in a fine, and Glenn wasn't the only lineman so punished. "Conduct unbecoming an offensive lineman" is a loose label under which almost any action or omission is subject to sanction. Most of the fine pool is distributed to charities at season's end.

That doesn't make it a charitable endeavor. When Glenn took the day off on October 26, 2000, to be with his wife, Maya, for the birth of their first child, Tarik Isiah, his linemates sympathized.

"We fined him," said center Jeff Saturday, Glenn's neighbor and ride to work, his closest friend on the team. "Ten bucks for missing meetings and another $10 for missing practice."

Not as Easy as It First Appeared

Edgerrin James was a rookie in 1999. He ran for 1,553 yards and 13 touchdowns. He won the league rushing title. The Colts won 11 games in succession. They went 13-3. They had a first-round bye, the first since they had moved to Indianapolis from Baltimore before the 1984 season.

"Everything was real easy and you would think it was going to happen every year," said James.

James continued to dominate in 2000, when he rambled 1,709 yards and again won the rushing title, but his eyes were opened. The Colts had to win their last three games to make the playoffs. They were knocked out in the first round by Miami.

Then James tore the anterior cruciate ligament in his left knee in 2001. Six games and 662 yards into the season, he was finished, and the road back in 2002 was no Sunday stroll. He struggled with ankle, rib and hamstring injuries.

All the while, players came and went, and the Colts achieved nothing during the postseason. James's was a more mature, more appreciative mindset in the midst of the 2003 playoffs.

"Now you understand that the locker room is totally different than it was back then," he said. "We've just got to make use of our opportunity to do what we've got to do."

Their Rims Weren't Always Chrome

Money is no object for NFL players, but most have done enough living to learn something about life before they signed one of those fat NFL contracts.

Wide receiver Troy Walters tooled around the Stanford campus in a 1989 Ford Tempo. David Thornton drives a Cadillac Escalade now; he had a 1993 Nissan Sentra during his schoolboy days at North Carolina.

Wide receiver Brandon Stokley had a 1991 Mazda 626 hatchback with more than 100,000 miles on it when he signed a free agent contract with Baltimore in 1999. He still was driving it two years later.

"I'm kind of a cheap guy," he acknowledged.

Former Colts cornerback Walt Harris drove to classes at Mississippi State in a red 1978 Toyota Corolla given him by a brother, at least until it broke down returning to Starkville from a visit to his LaGrange, Georgia, home. Harris abandoned the car alongside the road near Tuscaloosa, Alabama. It wasn't worth the price of a tow.

Left guard Rick DeMulling's pride was a 1967 full-size Chevy van his grandpa gave him. DeMulling still misses it.

He pulled the captain's chairs, replaced them with love seats and covered floor, ceiling and walls with brown shag carpet. An injured University of Idaho teammate acquired a handicapped parking pass. DeMulling and his buddies used the van as a rolling clubhouse between classes.

"It was trash. It was awesome," said DeMulling. "I absolutely loved it. My favorite car by far."

Former defensive lineman Chad Bratzke was raised conservatively and lives that way, just like Stokley.

When the New York Giants took Bratzke in the fifth round of the 1994 draft, he had his well-worn 1986 Camaro shipped to Giants Stadium from his Florida home. The Giants equipment manager stopped the transport driver when he attempted to offload Bratzke's car at the stadium. He couldn't conceive of a player having such a shabby set of wheels.

"A couple of girls I dated said, 'Wow. You have another car, don't you?'" Bratzke recalled. 'I knew real quick that wasn't the one for me."

Placekicker Mike Vanderjagt drove a 1991 Jeep Wrangler and sold shoes for five dollars an hour in Huntington, West Virginia, between graduating from West Virginia and signing with the CFL's Toronto Argonauts in 1996.

Defensive tackle Larry Triplett had a strong affection for his 1990 Jeep Cherokee. The same went for wide receiver Reggie Wayne and his 1993 Toyota Camry CE.

"It's a hooptee, a CE, bottom of the line, but it got me started," said Wayne. "You can't forget that. I don't go to the ball in it. I crank it up and just drive it around for a while."

Coach Tony Dungy knows the deal. He had heard the stories about the high draft choices who bought flashy cars and had them repossessed when they didn't make it. So when Dungy signed a free agent contract with Pittsburgh in 1977, he kept his beat up beater, a 1966 Buick LeSabre.

He drove it to his first game at Three Rivers Stadium. An attendant stopped him dead at the gate to the players' lot.

"My window won't roll up, so I've got plastic on the window and I show him my pass," said Dungy.

"'Where'd you find that pass? You can't be on the team,'" countered the attendant.

"I said, 'Please. You've got to let me in so I can play.'"

The attendant finally relented. So did Dungy. By midseason, he was driving a 1978 Thunderbird.

Tight end Marcus Pollard developed into a versatile offensive component and a vociferous Colt. (Robert Scheer/*The Indianapolis Star*)

Pollard Is Colts' "X" Factor

Tight end Marcus Pollard was an enormously important element of the Colts' offense and their ability to run it without benefit of huddling.

Pollard could line up tight and take on a defensive end or a linebacker in pass protection or the running game. Or, with his size (6'5", 247) and speed, he could set wide or in the slot and range over the middle or deep.

Bottom line, Pollard gave the Colts a tight end/wide receiver option without substituting. That helped make the no-huddle go.

Veteran Receiver a Nice Catch

Brandon Stokley signed as a free agent prior to the 2003 season, then missed most of the first 12 games with an assortment of injuries.

He proved worth waiting for.

He had seven catches for 95 yards and two touchdowns against Atlanta. He caught nine passes for 67 yards and the tying touchdown in a 20-17 victory at Houston that clinched the AFC South title. Then he exploded during the playoffs: four catches, 144 yards and two touchdowns against Denver; four receptions for 57 yards and a touchdown against Kansas City.

It was primary production from a No. 3 receiver.

"He's not a guy who's going to say, 'Throw me the ball,'" said five-time Pro Bowl wide receiver Marvin Harrison. "He could care less. He wants to win. He's going to block, run his routes full speed and he's never going to complain for the ball."

Harrison loved playing with Stokley. Stokley loved playing with Harrison.

While Harrison was occupying a cornerback and a safety on the outside, Stokley was streaking down the middle, creating havoc.

"He's the main weapon on this offense," said Stokley. "He opens things up for the rest of us."

Special Affinity for Special Teams

Marcus Pollard owed his football life to special teams. That's where he made it while transitioning from Bradley University basketball player to undrafted free agent professional football player.

But after nine years in the NFL, six as a starting tight end, Pollard was a long way from the kickoff team. He hadn't worked with the unit in three years. He didn't even know where to line up.

That didn't stop him from exhorting special teams coach Russ Purnell as the Colts' improbable comeback progressed during the fourth quarter of a 38-35 victory at Tampa Bay in 2003.

"Come on, Coach," Pollard insisted. "If somebody needs a blow, put me in there. I'll cover a kick."

Purnell shook him off. Pollard continued to campaign.

Finally, Purnell responded. With the scored tied at 35, 35 seconds on the clock and everyone's legs sapped by the long comeback and the thick Florida humidity, Purnell knew running back Ricky Williams wasn't ready to go, not after three fourth-quarter touchdown drives.

"Get in there for Ricky," Purnell barked at Pollard.

Teammates Detron Smith and Cliff Crosby told Pollard where to line up and what to do. Pollard did it. He sprinted down the hash, butted one blocker, shrugged another, then tackled return man Aaron Stecker after a five-yard return.

That play was Tony Dungy's favorite of an epic game. It was an example of the type of team chemistry for which one strives.

"Chemistry, to me, is all your guys feeling like the most important thing is winning," said Dungy. "When you have that, your chemistry is great."

That, as much as anything, was responsible for the Colts' 14-5 season.

Chapter Twelve

ETC., PART 2

Winning Close Games a Habit Worthy of Cultivation

It's noteworthy that one of the best regular seasons in Colts history began and ended in pretty much the same manner: With a hostile crowd on its feet, screaming, Mike Vanderjagt's field goals clearing the crossbar and the clock clicking toward 0:00.

Colts win.

It happened in Game 1, which Vanderjagt won, 9-6, with a 45-yard field goal with one second to play at Cleveland. It happened in Game 16, when Vanderjagt kicked a 43-yard field goal as time expired to beat Houston 20-17 at Reliant Field.

The Colts went 12-4 in 2003 largely because they learned to win the tight, tough games. The went 5-1 in games decided by three points or less.

That's why, when the Colts took over on their own 10-yard line with 2:40 to play at Houston, there was no sense of panic.

"You've been there before. You've made the plays before. You can make them again. It's not like anything had to be said in the huddle," offered Colts quarterback Peyton Manning, who directed the game-winning drive.

Making the plays becomes a habit.

"We did it because we had to do it," said rookie safety Donald Strickland, who returned his second NFL interception 19 yards to the Houston five to set up the tying touchdown.

Those Texans Were Snakebit

If you're looking for the beginning, you have to go back, way back, beyond Baltimore, beyond the Colts, to 1952 and the Dallas Texans. That woeful team's key players formed the core of the Colts.

After an 0-7 start, the pathetic Texans became wards of the league, which took them from owner Giles Miller, a Dallas businessmen, and moved them to Hershey, Pennsylvania. There, the Texans lost four of their last five games to finish 1-11.

Half the 40 players on the team's roster never played again. An even dozen, including future Pro Football Hall of Fame members Art Donovan and Gino Marchetti, became members of a new franchise founded by Carroll Rosenbloom in 1953, the Baltimore Colts.

The Colts would win the first of consecutive NFL championships only five years later, but Donovan recalls fondly some of the times he had with the ragamuffin Texans, who trained in Kerrville and employed a Mexican restaurant supervisor named Willie Garcia as their equipment manager.

"Willie had a wooden leg, and when a ball got kicked into the high grass, we'd make him go get it," laughed Donovan. "If there was a rattlesnake in there, he had only a one in two chance of getting bit on the leg."

Marchetti remembered one payday during the Texans' latter days in Dallas. Coach Jimmy Phelan called the players in before the day's workout began.

"He said, 'I'm not telling you these checks aren't any good,'" Marchetti recalled. "'But what I'm going to do is cancel practice right now.'

"You want to see 33 guys hustle? No showers. No anything. Straight to the bank."

The Colts celebrated their 65th season as NFL members in 2107.

Dungy Prefers Example to Chatter

Tony Dungy was a strong proponent of "in-your-face" defense but he prefers a quieter approach to the doctrine he holds most dear: his Christianity.

Dungy's approach to coaching, he said, "is based on the biblical perspective." He doesn't rant and belittle. He doesn't cuss and storm. His style is "stewardship." He leads by example, on the field, in his life.

"It's not, 'This is my life, and here is my religion,' with him," said punter Hunter Smith. "It's, 'Faith and Jesus are my life.'"

Colts owner Jim Irsay sees the same thing. He speaks of Dungy's "grace and dignity."

"He really reminds me of Tom Landry," said Irsay. "He was always very grounded in his personal beliefs and Tony's the same way. I think his upbringing and his spiritual foundation is why he's so steady, like Landry."

Dungy was raised in a Christian home, but his true "conversion" dates to St. Vincent College in Latrobe, Pennsylvania, site of the Pittsburgh Steelers' 1978 training camp.

Dungy was an undrafted free agent in his second season, still working to master his conversion from college quarterback to professional safety. He reported to camp, fitter, stronger, more studied and ready than ever in his career.

He came down with mononucleosis. He was confined to his room. He feared his release would be forthcoming.

"I was desperate and a little scared," recalled Dungy. "I was seeing my chances slip away."

Help came from Dungy's roommate, safety Donnie Shell, a four-year veteran who won four Super Bowls and was voted to the Pro Bowl five times as a Steeler.

"I think the Lord is just trying to get your attention," Shell told Dungy one evening. "Maybe this is too big. Maybe you've elevated it to first place in your life and it shouldn't be first place."

Dungy listened. He pondered. He prayed. He changed. He made a crucial decision the morning after his talk with Shell.

"It's a conscious decision," said Dungy. "You put your trust in the Lord. Your motivation changes. It's not what you do but why you do it and how you do it that becomes a little different."

So you continue to coach and expect "in-your-face" defense, but you don't live "in-your-face" Christianity.

"Scripture says, 'Let your light shine,'" volunteered Shell, now director of player development for the Carolina Panthers. "It doesn't say, 'Make it shine.'"

Larceny Must Be Learned

Over his first 15 years as an NFL defensive coordinator and head coach, coach Tony Dungy's teams averaged 21 interceptions and only three times had fewer than 18 in a season. Over his first two seasons in Indianapolis, the Colts totaled 25 interceptions.

Cornerback Nick Harper jumped into the league lead with three interceptions in the first two games of 2003, but despite a consistently productive pass rush, the Colts made only 12 more in their final 15 games.

No mystery to Dungy.

"We don't have interceptors," he said.

Dungy didn't consider the problem to be a matter of talent. He likened the Colts to Donnie Shell, whom he played alongside and later coached at Pittsburgh. Shell entered the league in 1974 as a stand-up defensive end/linebacker and was converted to safety. He had no experience in pass coverage, said Dungy, and poor hands, but he worked hard and he evolved.

By the time Shell retired after the 1987 season, he was the league's career leader for interceptions by a strong safety with 51.

"Some guys are natural playing the ball," said Dungy. "It's in their mind all the time; they think like receivers. Other guys don't. We've got to develop that."

Colts Trip Over "Hole" in the Rulebook

The no-huddle offense with which the Colts operated almost exclusively in 2003 was designed to do several things.

Wearing down a defense and preventing it from making situational substitutions are among them.

Of course the NFL is point-counterpoint, a chess match, a constant struggle to gain and edge, or to deny one. Too often, the Colts believe, opponents have countered by feigning injuries.

It happened during a victory at Tennessee, where Titans defensive linemen Albert Haynesworth and Robaire Smith seemed to alternate limping off one play, then returning the next. Each time, the clock was stopped, the offense's rhythm disrupted, and Tennessee was provided the opportunity to substitute fresh players best suited to the down and distance.

But the most crucial "injury" of the season came during a 38-34 loss to New England. With 1:09 to play and the Colts trailing 38-34 and facing a second and one at the New England nine-yard line, Patriots linebacker/end Willie McGinest went down clutching his left knee.

He returned after one play and, with 14 seconds on the clock, made the game-saving tackle on James at the two-yard line. McGinest celebrated by sprinting to midfield on his aggrieved knee.

If a team has no timeouts but suffers an injury to a player during the final two minutes of either half, it is granted an extra timeout. If the injury is suffered by the team on offense, 10 seconds are run off the clock. If the injured player is on defense, there is no runoff, and no penalty until a second injury, when a five-yard walk-off is required.

Tony Dungy called it a "hole in the rule."

"It's something we're going to have to look at," said Dungy. "It's hard for me to understand why the offense would be penalized in one situation and the defense gets a free one, but that's the way the rule reads."

Legislating the Fun out of Football

You might say the Colts had the early momentum. They grabbed it prior to kickoff.

With the kickoff team on the field and awaiting the go from television, Ricky Williams began rocking, swaying with the rap beat blaring from the loudspeakers. Then Williams was singing, "We're ready. We're ready. We're ready."

In a moment, 11 men swayed and sang as one.

"We just fed off it," said defensive back Donald Strickland, a member of the kickoff team. "It gave us a lot of energy. It gave the whole team a lot of energy."

That's a fact. The Colts on the sideline were pulled in. Members of the RCA Dome crowd stood and swayed.

The trigger had been pulled on the Colts' 38-7 trampling of the Atlanta Falcons.

The NFL deemed the pre-kickoff swaying by the Colts' coverage unit in 2003 as "taunting." (Matt Kryger/**The Indianapolis Star**)

"It started with them, their dancing," said running back Edgerrin James.

"I think that was the key moment," offered tight end Marcus Pollard, who watched with James from the sideline. "Everybody kind of decided, 'This thing's for real. Let's kick it off and put one on them.' That set the tone for the rest of the game."

It won't happen again. The NFL cut in on this dance.

The league deemed it "taunting" and announced during the March 2004 owners meetings that any further instance would result in a 15-yard penalty. Mike Pereira, the league's director of officiating, said unsportsmanlike conduct and taunting would be points of emphasis in 2004, and the Colts' ritual falls in that category.

"I think it's taunting," he said. "It's 31-nothing and they're doing it."

Of course they were doing it when it was 0-0, on the opening kickoff.

"Then it's offensive," countered Pereira. "It's a group demonstration and that's not going to be allowed."

And that's that.

"It was fun while it lasted," said owner Jim Irsay.

Simpler Can Be Better

The Cover-2 defense that Tony Dungy brought to the Colts and defensive coordinator Ron Meeks oversaw was many things, simple chief amongst them.

Safety Idrees Bashir estimated that the Colts ran "at least" 35 coverages in 2001, when Vic Fangio coordinated the defense and Jim Mora was head coach. That number, Bashir volunteered, was reduced to about 10 by Dungy and Meeks.

"It was like going from Harvard to a Division III school," Bashir said.

That's a fact, confirmed Dungy.

"I've always said, 'If you can count to three, you can play in this defense," said Dungy. "If you can count to three fast, you can play it well.'"

"Cover-2" refers to the two safeties, who play deep in an effort to take away the over-the-top pass, the game-breaking play. Players are responsible for a single gap, and the scheme is based on zone pass coverage. That allows defenders to "face up," see the football and swarm to it, which produces gang-tackling, deflections, interceptions.

What it didn't produce was shut-down efficiency. In their second season in the defense, the Colts ranked 20th in points allowed (21.0), tied for 20th against the run (123.8 yards a game) and 18th in stopping third down conversions (38.3 percent). They yielded 100-yard days to seven rushers.

Neither the talent nor the proficiency were where Dungy wanted it, but a look back to 2001 is instructive. The Colts gave up 30.4 points a game—486 points in all—the fourth most generous yield in league history.

"Nike Generation" Has a Few Things to Learn

Multimillionaires barely old enough to vote are a phenomenon of modern sport, one that can produce people whose bankrolls far outstrip their experience, and sometimes their judgment.

"I refer to it as the 'Nike Generation,'" said then-Colts running backs coach Gene Huey. "They can afford to go around the world, but they haven't taken time to explore it. That comes through age. That comes through trial and error. That comes through ups and downs and being able to make adjustments.

"That comes through just living."

An Elite Fraternity that Shares a Special Bond

Former Colts defensive line coach John Teerlinck told his players that there are 50 U.S. senators, but only 32 NFL defensive line coaches. Theirs is an elite fraternity, a brotherhood bound by common highs, lows and striving, and too-frequent firings.

Linebackers coach Mike Murphy knew the deal and appreciates it.

"I have a lot of great friends, and if I had a heart attack on the field, there would probably be 1,000 condolences and 5,000 job applications," said Murphy. "You have one of the premier jobs in the country. It's hard to get, and it's harder to hold."

Murphy coached 19 years in the NFL—the last six with the Colts—before he reached a conference championship game. He relished the Colts' run to the 2003 AFC finale.

"People ask why you coach," volunteered Murphy. "It's the feeling afterward, in the locker room. If you were Bill Gates, and you had all the money in the world, you couldn't buy the feeling you have in the locker room after Tampa, after the second Denver game, after the Kansas City game."

Coaching Offers Few Guarantees

Former offensive line coach Howard Mudd knew that feeling, and he knew disappointment. He started in the NFL as a player in 1964. He was one of the best in the business. He had been to a conference title game twice prior to 2003.

"One was 'The Drive,'" said Mudd. "The other was 'The Fumble.'"

Thirty years. Two conference title games. Four words to describe them. The NFL is a tough business.

"The Drive" was a John Elway-directed march that covered 98 yards and enabled Denver to tie the 1986 AFC championship game in the final minute. The Broncos then beat Cleveland in overtime, 23-20. In a rematch a year later, Cleveland appeared ready to take its turn in the Super Bowl. Then Browns running back Ernest Byner fumbled at the Denver three-yard line with little more than a minute to play. "The Fumble." The Broncos won again, 38-33.

Mudd was Cleveland's offensive line coach.

Lots of Legends; Only One Hero

Ron Meeks, the Colts' former defensive coordinator from 2002 to 2008, is the ninth of 14 children. Five were by his father's previous marriage, but Ron grew up in a three-bedroom house in Jacksonville, Florida, with eight brothers and sisters. It made for tight quarters. It made for a tight family.

Spencer Meeks was a mail carrier. His wife, Florestine, was a nurse. Spencer worked mornings, Florestine evenings, so there almost always was a parent at home, at school activities, at games, at the childrens' sides.

Ron went on to play football at Arkansas State and in the CFL. He coached under Larry Lacewell, Jimmy Johnson, Dave Wannstedt, Dave Campo, Dan Reeves, Rich Brooks, Norv Turner, Ray Rhodes, Mike Martz, Lovie Smith and now Tony Dungy. He has been around bunches of good coaches and great players, but his hero died in 1997, when death took Spencer Meeks unexpectedly.

Dad was Ron's coach, scoutmaster, playmate and workmate. Every Saturday throughout Ron's youth, they arose at 6 a.m., sorted and packed laundry for 10 and headed for the laundromat. A couple hours later, they would be home, stringing all those clean clothes on a clothesline that ran from one end of the family's double lot to the other.

Ron went to the Super Bowl with Atlanta in 1998 and again with St. Louis in 2001. He ached for his father to be with him.

"One of the biggest disappointments of my life," said Ron, his eyes fixed on something far distant. "My father didn't get a chance to see me in the Super Bowl. I always wanted my father to see me at the Super Bowl."

Keep Your Eye on What Matters

Tom Moore's career in the NFL included 21 seasons as an offensive coordinator with three teams, the last 11 with the Colts. He carries with him one of the best bits of advice he ever received, from Hall of Fame Pittsburgh coach Chuck Noll, with whom Moore won two Super Bowl rings.

"Don't major in the minors," Noll told Moore.

"That's still right," said Noll, who won four Super Bowls with the Steelers. "You focus on what's important."

No Missing the Missed Tackles

Tony Dungy considered three or four missed tackles a good game. In the Colts' overtime loss to Carolina in 2003, they had two dozen.

Episodes of sloppy tackling are not characteristic of the Colts alone. All around the NFL the mutters are audible: tackling is becoming a lost art.

"I think it kind of goes in cycles," said Dungy. "But I think as the league has become more of a passing league; we're spending more time on pass defense and coverages and schemes, and we are spending less time on fundamentals. I think there are still some very good tacklers in the league, and good tackling teams. But I'd say on the whole, if you look at all the teams, it probably has gone downhill since the advent of all the passing."

A lot goes into it, but it's primarily a matter of emphasis, of practice. Roster limits, salary cap constraints, injured reserve rules and the 16-game schedule all contribute. Neither college nor professional teams hit in practice like they did when Dungy was a player during the late 1970s and early 1980s.

Once the season is underway, the emphasis is on avoiding injury, keeping fresh legs. The Colts, like most league teams, seldom practice in pads. It's helmets only. No tackling.

"We had no idea what no pads meant. Never heard of it," said Dungy, who played safety for the 1978 world champion Pittsburgh Steelers. "We had live goal lines on Friday. That's all we knew."

Dungy recalls a practice hit Steelers safety Donnie Shell put on wide receiver Louis Lipps.

"I didn't know if Lipps was ever going to play again," said Dungy. "The offensive coaches would get mad. The defensive coaches would say, 'We want to go for the ball, but let's relax a bit.'

"Practices were pretty heated and spirited. Dick Vermeil, in fact, who was notorious for his tough practices, when he started broadcasting he came to one of our practices, and he said, 'Wow.'"

Still, Dungy's Tampa Bay teams were considered good tacklers. He considers it a matter of personnel and mindset. Faced with choosing between a safety or cornerback with great coverage skills and great tackling skills, Dungy will take the tackler.

He believes a team can achieve and maintain tackling proficiency without a lot of hitting.

"It's more reprogramming yourself to use your shoulder pads, get your body in position," said Dungy. "It's not a punishment like we're going to have nutcracker drills or anything like that."